Praise for *Real W*

Socialism thrives under conditions of mass ignorance, invariably leading to misery, moral decay, and human bondage. To its acolytes, such a statement is dismissed as sweeping platitude, but Dr. Gerard Lameiro's scholarly research and thoughtful analysis presents the dreadful facts of socialism as a veritable set of economic laws.

Despite centuries of evidence substantiating the free and voluntary exchange of goods and services – capitalism – as the most powerful antidote to poverty and political subjugation, Dr. Lameiro explains how the seductive allure of socialism comes to destroy once-prosperous nations. *Real World Socialism* is an important book that arms its readers with intellectual clarity necessary in rolling back the frontiers of ignorance.

Bob Schaffer
Headmaster, Liberty Common School, Fort Collins, CO
Past Chairman, Colorado State Board of Education
Former Member, U. S. House of Representatives (CO – 4)

Dr. Lameiro has done it again. A powerful, thought provoking read that answers the big question we all are asking ..."what's going on?" You won't just read the book; you'll end up writing in the margins. Get two of these books, one for yourself and one to give to a friend. After reading this book, like me, you'll say "AMEN".

Perry Atkinson
President/CEO
theDove Radio & TV Network

I think that **Real World Socialism** should be the primary textbook in any class on world history, economics and government policy. I see and hear, far too often, our young people leaving college with an eye on socialist ideals. They have been indoctrinated ...

Mark Hahn
Drive Time Live
KSCJ, Sioux City, IA

Our nation is under attack from those who want to destroy and replace everything that we value. This is not a time to stand silent and unprepared. Dr. Lameiro's book will give you facts, specifics ... the ammunition that you need ... to battle all socialist lies and false promises.

Larry Conners
Talk Radio Host
Larry Conners USA

In this book, perennial optimist, Dr. Gerard Lameiro shows his side as a realist. He helps those who are still being seduced by socialism to understand that even if it were free, it would never be worth it.

Karen Kataline
Commentator, Columnist & Talk Show Host

America's bootheels are on the edge of the cliff and the socialists are trying to push us into the abyss. Read and understand what Dr. Lameiro is telling us ... this man <u>knows</u> what he's talking about!

Zeb Bell
"Zeb at the Ranch" Radio
Murtaugh, ID

Dr. Lameiro's new book, ***Real World Socialism: Spiritual, Moral and Economic Bankruptcy - Sold by Using False Hopes and Deceit***, is both timely and powerful! Socialism was once a dirty word in America. But today, the Left embraces and endorses socialism with enthusiasm. Dr. Lameiro not only explains socialism from an historical perspective, but he makes it relevant to our time. He makes a powerful case for the freedom, opportunity, and prosperity that capitalism provides. This book will give you a greater understanding of how political and economic freedom go hand-in-hand and what is at stake in America. Dr. Lameiro's writing style makes complex issues clear and interesting. This is a must read!

George Landrith
President, Frontiers of Freedom Institute
Host, Conservative Commandoes

Nobody understands socialism better than Dr. Lameiro. Anyone who wants to save our country or those that proclaim the wonders of socialism need to read this book, before our beloved land of freedom and opportunity is dismantled. You'll learn the true goals of socialism, methods to bring it about, and the end result of carnage. It's not too late, as Dr. Lameiro provides a road map ensuring that we will remain a beacon of freedom for future generations and the world.

Erskine
Nationally Syndicated, Talk Radio Host

Dr. Lameiro is my show's #1 Fan Favorite and most trusted analyst because he is the most accurate analyst in the industry, in not only predicting outcomes of elections, but also in predicting trends. Plus, he delivers it in his unique upbeat, compelling and easy-to-understand style!

In *Real World Socialism,* Dr. Lameiro uses his unparalleled skills and experience to address the rising scourge of socialism in America, and in the way only Dr. Lameiro can do. He takes the reader back to understand the truthful history of socialism and its failures, as well as the tactics being used to manipulate Americans into transforming America into a socialist system, and what that will mean to us all.

This is the book the mainstream media and the socialist-supporting academic institutions don't want Americans to read, and why every American needs to, before it's too late

Andrea Kaye
Host/Executive Producer
The Andrea Kaye Show, The Answer San Diego/Salem Media

In his new book *Real World Socialism,* one of my favorite guests, Dr. Gerard Lameiro, brilliantly lays out the pitfalls of socialism and how it leads to the decay of a society – morally, spiritually, and economically. This book is a great rebuttal to those who think "Socialism hasn't worked because WE haven't tried it yet."

Charlie James
Morning Show Host
AM 1250 WTMA, Charleston, SC

Socialists in universities, the media and politics have been deceived and are deceiving the youth about the real dangers of socialism. Dr Gerard Lameiro's *Real World Socialism* is a bright wake-up, light-of-truth in the dark abyss of cultural failures in history. Of all the hundreds of book reviews we've done, there are none more perceptive and prescient than the prophet of our times, Dr Gerard Lameiro. We highly recommend him to all who care about our future.

Bob & Geri Boyd
Hosts/Producers
Issues in Education, issues@cableone.net
Bob Boyd
President, National Association of Christian Educators

There is no one better suited to discuss the toxic nature of socialism than Dr. Lameiro. He offers a guide to effectively presenting the case for capitalism, free markets and democratic political systems. Socialism is replete with failure, misery, abject poverty, and the suppression of freedom. Dr. Lameiro offers the insights that make the case against socialism and for freedom. A must read!!

Mike Siegel
Talk Radio Host

Dr Lameiro has been an incredible prognosticator relative to America's mood. He stands alone in predicting future behavior of the American Voter. Plus, he is a Great American.

Bill Cunningham
Nationally Syndicated, Talk Radio Host
Premiere Radio Network

I heartily recommend Dr Lameiro's new book, given the nature of his work to date. Anyone who can predict the outcome of an election, using such scientific and methodical accuracy has my interest. Dr L has such a unique perspective which fascinates young and old alike. His take on any given situation is amazing to behold, which adds to his value as a writer, speaker and guest.

Xander Gibb
Writer, International Political Commentator and Broadcaster
Host, The Xander Gibb Show
London

Dr. Lameiro has outdone himself once again. His brand new book *Real World Socialism* is a tour de force of socialist experiments and socialist rhetoric. Dr. Lameiro takes on not only Karl Marx and Friedrich Engels on Marxism and scientific socialism, but also addresses a rather complete spectrum of variations of socialism that the world has encountered over the last 300 years. It is an in-depth panoply of why socialism always fails in theory and in practice. If you ever need to defend America, freedom and capitalism against the grandiose promises, subtle deceit, and spurious claims of socialism, this is your book. It also makes a great gift for your high school or college student facing the on-campus bias of the Left.

Barry Farber
Nationally Known, Talk Radio Legend

Real World Socialism

Spiritual, Moral and Economic Bankruptcy – Sold By
Using False Hopes and Deceit

Gerard Lameiro, Ph.D.

Author of *Great News for America*
Popular TV and Talk Radio Show Personality
"America's #1 Political Analyst"

For more information on the author, his books, blog posts, speaking engagements, and consulting services, please visit the author's website: GreatNewsForAmerica.com.

Cover Design and Interior Book Design by MDW Graphics & Type, mdwgraphics.com.

First Edition.

Available from Amazon.com and other retail outlets.

Available on Kindle and other devices.

This book is dedicated to millions of Americans and millions more people around the world who want to understand socialism.

My hope is that they can avoid the pain and suffering, poverty and destitution, torture and murder that millions have suffered under the various forms of socialism in the last 300 years.

Contents

Chapter 1

What is Socialism?

Socialism always leads on a path to spiritual, moral, and economic bankruptcy. But, sometimes actual bankruptcy is avoided by adopting free market and capitalist principles before it is too late. Then, it can no longer be called socialism; it's capitalism that's running the nation in question.

Indeed, socialism has a long and tortuous record of failures as we will highlight. For those reasons and more, it's important to understand socialism

This book will focus on the reality of socialism, its characteristics, and why it consistently fails. It will also provide actual examples of socialist experiments that have failed miserably. Finally, it will discuss why the arguments for socialism fail both in theory and in practice.

Let's first turn our attention to the names used to describe socialism.

Socialism and Its Variations

Socialism has existed in various forms and under a variety of different names for hundreds of years.

Besides the name socialism, its characteristics show up under the terms Marxism, scientific socialism, democratic socialism, social democracy, progressive socialism, designer socialism, Christian socialism, market socialism, National Socialism,

Nazism, fascism, communism, totalitarianism, Scandinavian socialism, and also the kibbutzim (plural of kibbutz) socialist communities that pre-dated Israel's War of Independence (1948 – 1949).[1]

"Scandinavian Socialism" – Examples of Welfare States Funded by Capitalism

Of course, some caution needs to be exercised with the names used for socialism. To illustrate, consider the Scandinavian country of Sweden with its so-called socialist society. Rather than an example of socialism, it might better be described as a welfare state funded by capitalism.[2]

Sweden became a welfare state by using up much of its capital, accumulated over years of living under economic freedom and the associated economic productivity that such freedom generated. But, with Sweden's high taxes and burdensome regulations used to feed their snowballing welfare state, Sweden's capital was eventually dissipated to the point where economic growth was dramatically curtailed, and their economy was significantly damaged.[3]

Denmark, another Scandinavian country, followed a similar path. With a marginal income tax rate of 55.6% on incomes equaling or exceeding $55,000, a national sales tax of 25%, an automobile purchase tax of a staggering 180%, plus other taxes, the effective Danish tax rate was about 70%.[4]

In recent years, the so-called Scandinavian socialist nations have had to retrench and move more toward free market capitalism out of sheer economic necessity.[5]

Thus, it's doubtful then that the Scandinavian socialist nations that so many hold up as democratic socialist models of utopian success, were ever anything more than capitalist-funded welfare states.[6]

Returning to the many different labels for socialism listed earlier in this chapter, one conclusion is obvious. Every implementation of socialism over the years did not exhibit every attribute of socialism in the same way and to the same degree.

Yet, in all these variations and despite numerous monikers, certain traits usually showed up in attempts at governing under socialism or adopting socialist policies in a given country. What are these traits, and importantly, what is the core attribute of socialism?

Socialism is a Secular Religion

First, socialism is essentially and effectively a secular religion that fundamentally conflicts with, and also often directly attempts to compete with, Western Civilization and its Judeo-Christian heritage (even if all of its advocates are not fully aware of the competition or even the inherent conflict itself). This is its first and most important attribute.[7]

Socialism's long history is largely anti-Jewish, anti-Christian, anti-family, and anti-private property. It usually seeks to erase and to eradicate God and the Old and New Testaments of the Bible from the minds and hearts of people. Take, for example, the attempts in the United States to eliminate the Ten Commandments from display in courthouses.[8] Or, consider another example, the efforts to remove the statement "In God We Trust" from our currency.[9]

Socialism also attempts to stifle God and the Bible as the inspirational source of spiritual and moral guidance for people. Socialism tries to replace the God of the Bible with the false god of government. Why?

God, Human Dignity, Individual Freedom, and Morality in Our Judeo-Christian Heritage

The fundamental reason why socialism is at war with God and our Judeo-Christian heritage is simple. Our faith tradition believes in God and the human dignity we all share as children of God. From this human dignity, it follows that individuals have both freedom and morality.

In the Jewish and Christian faith traditions, individual freedom and morality are inextricably linked to God, and indeed, form the DNA of our Judeo-Christian heritage. Without morality, there can be no freedom. Without freedom, there can be no morality.

Morality is the understanding of what human actions are good and what human actions are evil. If there is no morality, there is no freedom to choose between a good human action and an evil human action because the moral distinction between good and evil does not exist.

Similarly, if there is no freedom and mankind must choose only one human action in a given situation because of government dictates, morality doesn't effectively exist.

Certainly, no moral decision can be made freely, if government is in complete control.

Much has been written about God, our human dignity, individual freedom, and morality beyond the scope of this chapter. For one discussion, please see my 2014 book: *Renewing America and Its Heritage of Freedom.*[10]

Returning to the question of why socialism is at war with the Jewish and Christian faith traditions and is constantly attacking Judaism and Christianity, we see the reason rather clearly. Faith in God, along with faith in the Jewish faith tradition, and faith in the Christian faith tradition, all believe in, and promote, and defend human dignity, individual freedom, and morality.

According to these faith traditions, God is in charge of all life on the earth and is the ultimate authority. God created Eternal Law, Divine Law, Natural Law, and expects Human Law to be consistent with God's laws.[11] The Judeo-Christian traditions also believe God will judge all human actions and will reward the good with life in an eternal paradise we call heaven.

Socialism Emerged Out of Atheism and Seeks a Secular Nation

In sharp contrast, socialism emerged out of atheism[12] and seeks to create a secular nation wherever it tries to put down its venomous roots. Socialists believe that the true god is the government and that the socialist policies they want to enact will create a human paradise on earth.

5

With socialism, socialists believe there is no need to wait for a future paradise in heaven; utopia can be obtained in this earthly world now, if only we adopt socialist policies.[13]

Human dignity, individual freedom, and morality all directly conflict with implementing socialism, despite any claims that advocates of socialism make to the contrary. For example, human dignity would not permit the torture and mass killings of millions of people around the world, who became victims to socialist tyranny (which often started out with so-called good intentions and grandiose promises of an earthly utopia.)

Another example of how socialist policies oppose human dignity is legally permitting babies to die with no attempt to save the baby's life, after a failed abortion results in a live birth. This policy is clearly infanticide and conflicts with the Judeo-Christian principle of human dignity.[14]

Why does socialism and the advocates of socialist policies wage war on God and the Jewish and Christian religions? The reasons are that both socialist proponents and socialist governments need to curtail individual freedom and circumvent morality, if they want to get, keep, and wield power over a nation.

Socialists need power to control a nation. That's why they attack God, religious freedom, religious expression, and both the Jewish faith and Christianity. Socialists cannot allow faith-based principles to stifle their ruthless and immoral actions to control a nation.

Socialism Sells False Hopes

Second, another characteristic of socialism is that it sells itself by making false hopes for a man-made utopia on earth delivering all human needs required by citizens, while allowing everyone to work in jobs they choose (or allowing some people not to work at all, again if they so choose). Socialists also frequently offer the false promises of complete fairness, justice and freedom as a result of equality.

In a socialist country, everyone in theory gets the same wages, the same goods and services, the same requirements of life, and the same benefits. In reality, those in the governing hierarchy of a socialist regime live an abundant lifestyle, at the same time that the rest of the nation's citizens are left in relative poverty.

To socialists, equality means equal outcomes for everyone, but certainty not equal opportunities for everyone to flourish. However, the equality stops with everyday citizens. The governing elite live in relative luxury and abundance, while all the others subsist in relative deprivation.

Socialism Delivers Poverty and Limits Freedom

All the while selling these lofty pledges to the people, socialism actually delivers abject poverty, injustice, and limits or eliminates human freedom. This is the third attribute of socialism.

As we mentioned above, equality in pragmatic terms turns out to be everyone shares in an equal level of poverty, a least for the vast majority of citizens.

Rationing and shortages of vital goods and services make equality essentially meaningless. For example, "Medicare for All" might sound like a tempting political promise to garner some votes during an election cycle to those unfamiliar with socialism and socialized medicine. But, if you have to wait months for a life-saving surgery as a result of a shortage of doctors and surgeons, then the "Medicare for All" promise rings rather hollow. Shortages, rationing, and long waiting lines for health care services are common in nations living with the limitations of socialized medicine.[15]

The bottom line is pretty straight forward. Socialism has been tried in many ways, at many different times, in many different places around the world over the last 300 years. In every instance, it has not only failed to achieve its stated hopes or goals or lies, but it has failed miserably.

Socialism in Some Cases Uses Torture and Murder to Enforce Policies

Worse than not achieving its overblown promises, socialism has destroyed economies, created economic misery, and also produced considerable abject poverty. It has forced many citizens from their homes to attempt to control their sinking economies with so-called needed relocations. Socialists, in their barbarous efforts to control populations under their power and control, have even brutally tortured and violently murdered millions of innocent people over the decades to enforce their socialist policies.[16] [17]

In addition, while making grandiose promises that will never be kept, socialism frequently tends to degrade into tyranny in its attempts to attain its bogus socialist goals.

Venezuela – Example of Democratic Socialism as a Gateway into a Totalitarian Dictatorship

The reason why socialism often is a gateway into a totalitarian dictatorship is that socialism requires power to control its citizens. Government control is typically needed to impose its so-called goal of equal economic outcomes on the entire population. Violating the human dignity of its citizens is a direct result of imposing the same power and control on its population.

When socialist policies fail to produce the results sought by the State, power and control continue to ratchet up, while individual freedoms are simultaneously stifled. Eventually, a totalitarian dictatorship is often the consequence.

To illustrate that last point, consider the example of Venezuela. Once the largest economy in Latin America, Venezuela collapsed financially under the strains of socialism.

In 1998, Hugo Chavez ran and was elected as a democratic socialist.[18] But, quickly thereafter, he emerged as a driven socialist leader. Subsequently, he developed into a totalitarian dictator, nationalizing a substantial portion of Venezuela's economy along the way. Under his version of socialism, Chavez:

> "expropriated six million hectares of land, the steel sector, cement sector, supermarkets, telecoms, banks,

dairy factories, coffee processing factories, hotels, and essentially ran all of them into the ground,"[19]

Hugo Chavez also instituted price controls, an offbeat, two-tiered system of currency exchange rates, and ineffective centralized planning. The economic results were disastrous. Venezuela suffered from hyperinflation as well as critical food and medical shortages. [20] [21]

According to one joint university study in Venezuela reported in 2018, the average Venezuelan lost 24 lbs. of body weight in the past year and about 90% of its citizens lived in poverty, a far cry from their affluent, oil-rich days before becoming a socialist country.[22]

Whether initiated by good intentions, bad intentions, power-hungry politicians, conceited intellectuals, pie-in-the-sky academics, or misguided do-gooders, socialism has always been, and will continue to remain, a complete and utter spiritual, moral, political, and economic failure.

Why does socialism always fail so consistently, despite all its various forms, and despite hiding behind all of its myriad list of names, and despite all of its glowing promised benefits? The answer lies in the fourth characteristic of socialism.

Socialism Violates Human Nature

Fourth, the direct answer to the question of why socialism consistently fails in the real world is that socialism violates human nature.[23] A religious, cultural, political, or economic system that is composed of human beings cannot hope to succeed in reality for long, if it openly violates human nature.

10

Two important attributes of human nature are competition and motivation. Human beings naturally compete in life. Children compete in childhood ball games and board games. High school students take SAT and ACT tests to compete with other students to gain acceptance into the best colleges and universities. Men and women compete in dating and social situations to find a lifelong spouse. People in the workforce not only compete for salary and wage increases on a regular basis, but they also compete for job promotions to improve their overall situations in life.[24]

Competition is ubiquitous, pervasive, and an integral part of human nature. More generally, competition even seems indigenous in the larger animal kingdom as well, where animals compete with one another for scarce food and other needs of life. Competition seems to exist naturally in life.

Socialism ignores the reality of competition in human nature. It expects people will all be completely content to receive the same pay, the same housing, the same medical care, the same food, the same everything in their lives.

Actually, it's worse than that. Socialism expects people will not only be content sharing equally in all resources, but it also assumes they will be content to share in equally low pay, equally poor housing, equally rationed health care shortages, equally unavailable food shortages, and equally shared poverty.

Socialism ignores the attribute in human nature that empowers and enervates much of human action, namely, motivation.

11

Motivation is the other big attribute of human nature socialism ignores. If nothing a person does can improve his or her life or their children's lives, they have little or no motivation to take that action. Without the ability to compete and get ahead, why would someone have the motivation to take a risk or expend some extra energy on a given task?

Let's consider an example. Suppose we have a candy bar manufacturing plant in a socialist country that has 1,000 factory workers, who are each paid the same low wage per day. None of the 1,000 workers have any incentive to do an outstanding job or to boost production by 10% or more on any given day. Their motivation is equally low.

Further, in our candy bar example, suppose a few workers are goofing off and the other average workers notice that fact. The workers, who are more productive, think it's totally unfair. Their pay is the same as the other workers, who are not producing as much. In this case, we have a demotivation problem and candy bar production might actually decrease dramatically. The better workers cut down on their level of production because their motivation and morale are zapped.

It's just human nature at work. Why work as hard as, or harder than, workers who goof off and get paid the exact same wage?

By ignoring human nature in general, and competition and motivation in particular, socialism fails repeatedly and consistently in all the experiments socialists try.

The Bottom Line

All the various forms of socialism operating under all the numerous labels used by socialists share several attributes, even though those traits might not at first be obvious.

Socialism is essentially and effectively a secular religion that emerged out of atheism and seeks the creation of a secular nation (or sometimes a secular global community). It fundamentally conflicts with, and also often directly attempts to compete with, Western Civilization and its Judeo-Christian heritage.

Socialism sells and promotes its ideas by making grandiose promises and generating false hopes among citizens of a socialist utopian paradise on earth. Yet, it consistently fails to deliver on its promises, hopes, and lies to the citizens. Rather, its policies typically result in shortages, rationing, and long waiting lines for necessary goods and services.

In the process of attempting to wield power over, and to control, its citizens, socialism seems to frequently lead to tyranny and often socialists resort to using torture and murder to enforce its policies.

Socialism usually fails because it violates human nature. Socialism culminates in at least reduced economic growth in some cases, but more often than not, it ends in poverty and destitution for a nation.

Socialism always leads on a path to spiritual, moral, and economic bankruptcy. But, sometimes actual bankruptcy is avoided by adopting free market and capitalist principles before it is too late.

Chapter 2

What are Examples of Socialism prior to the 20th Century?

Prior to the 20th century, variations of socialism showed up in two places – in the minds of thinkers and philosophers, as well as in actual socialist efforts to implement socialist experiments or to revolutionize existing governments in order to create socialist nations.

The early socialist thinkers as we discuss below largely designed idealistic or utopian models for governments that were never tried in the real world. Their concepts of how a government might be organized did, however, survive and seemed to permeate future socialist experiments or eventual socialist nations.

As we go through the various examples of socialist theory and practice in this book, along with the details of socialism and its impact on a nation's culture, politics, and economics, we will usually refer to all variations of socialist nations, socialist characteristics, and socialist policies as instances of socialism.

The reasons for this is that while different variations might appear unique, all the variations of socialist experiments and socialist nations tend to share the same traits outlined in Chapter 1. For example, socialism and communism share so much in common that it's more direct to consider communism another variation of socialism. Karl Marx, too, considered the final and ultimate end state of socialism to be communism.

To take one other illustration, socialism and democratic socialism also move a nation in the same governing direction so that there is little need to distinguish the two from one another. In other words, an advocate for democratic socialism is most likely also an advocate for socialism, and vice-versa.

Some socialists also believe that using a different label for socialism will help sell it to citizens, who ordinarily would reject outright socialism or even certain leftist policies, such as socialized medicine. For example, calling a comprehensive platform of governing policies "democratic socialism" might be more palatable and acceptable to some citizens, rather than calling the same platform "socialism."

Some advocates for socialism will also argue that one variation of socialism is different than, or better than, another variation of socialism. But, for those individuals, who believe in individual freedom and liberty, all forms of socialism fall into a singular bucket that generally opposes God, human dignity, individual freedom, and morality. In other words, the differences between some variations of socialism are more cosmetic than substantive.

It's worth noting as well that some forms of socialism exist as totalitarian regimes, while some instances of socialist governments permit some level of individual freedom. The mix of individual freedom vs. the government's freedom can vary quite a bit, all the way up to and including, complete totalitarian dictatorship. But, the momentum in socialist nations is normally toward totalitarianism because socialism fails without power, control, coercion, compulsion, and/or violence. Socialism moves toward totalitarianism customarily.

Let's turn our attention now to Plato and some of the other early socialist thinkers.

Plato (Author of the *Republic*) – An Early Socialist Thinker

Plato is probably the most well-known of all philosophers throughout history. His book, the *Republic,*[25] presents a utopian model for the ideal city, although Plato himself believed this idealistic endeavor could never be achieved for practical reasons.[26]

The *Republic* is a remarkable exercise in developing an ideal government. In a sense, the *Republic* anticipated future socialist experiments and future nations living under the various forms of socialism. It's also possible that Plato actually influenced those future advocates of socialism, giving them ideas to try out in the real world during subsequent generations. What were some of the features of Plato's ideal city?

For one thing, it was a class-based society composed of three distinct groups. The first of these groups were called the Guardians. Guardians were the ruling elite in Plato's *Republic*. Some of them were also called philosopher-kings. They were the best and brightest citizens, who had years of education and training. They were committed to doing the best for the ideal city. The second of these groups were termed the Auxiliaries. This group was empowered to support the Guardians as warriors for the *Republic.* Finally, the third group in this class-based society was the Producers, who carried out the day-to-day work of the ideal city, such as farmers and craftsmen.[27]

Other characteristics Plato proposes for his utopian model include a form of eugenics to develop the best citizens for the ideal city and regulations about arranged marriages, families, and a government nursery for raising children. In the *Republic,* Guardians would only marry other Guardians, Auxiliaries would only marry other Auxiliaries, and if a Producer (also called an Artisan) were born to a Guardian or an Auxiliary arranged marriage, the newly born Artisan would be raised with other Artisans.[28]

Still other features of this so-called ideal city include the use of euthanasia to help maintain "the purity of the race"[29] and the elimination of private property among the Guardians and Auxiliaries to keep these classes focused on their important duties to the *Republic.[30]*

Plato's *Republic* was certainly not advocating freedom and liberty, nor was it proposing a form of democracy either. The ideal city was really a totalitarian state that controlled individuals and made individual needs subordinate to the needs of the government.[31]

Plato's *Republic* written about 380 BC did offer future socialist thinkers ideas for constructing socialist nations. Unfortunately, those schemes didn't benefit individuals that might eventually be impacted by their implementation. They also didn't articulate the vital importance of individual freedom and morality.

Sir Thomas More (Author of *Utopia*) – Thought by Many to be a Socialist Thinker

Another early socialist thinker was Sir Thomas More, the Catholic martyr and saint, who was executed because he did not accept King Henry VIII as the head of the Church of England, believing instead in papal supremacy. The dispute over Church authority occurred when King Henry VIII chose to divorce his wife Catherine of Aragon to marry Anne Boleyn in violation of Catholic Church doctrine.[32]

Sir Thomas More is also the author of another well-known book, first published in 1516, called *Utopia* that has been praised by socialists over the years. In fact, the term "utopia" was actually coined by Sir Thomas More. *Utopia,* in fact, is a detailed description of a fictional perfect society that in many ways foreshadowed 20th century communism. Lenin, the Russian dictator, even thought so highly of *Utopia* that he honored Sir Thomas More along with Karl Marx and sixteen others on a monument in Moscow's Alexandrosky Garden.[33]

Incidentally, the word utopia in Greek means "no place" and the narrator's name in the book *Utopia*, is Hythlodaeus, which translates into "dispenser of nonsense."[34] While socialists have long given this book accolades, one wonders given those translations whether Sir Thomas More actually wrote the totalitarian tract as a satire, rather than as a model for a perfect socialist society.

Let's look now at *Utopia* in more detail.

What characterizes Sir Thomas More's perfect state of Utopia? First of all, Utopia is centrally planned in extraordinarily fine detail. The layout and distances among cities is rigidly planned. Hospitals are located in key places to meet citizens' needs for medical care.[35]

Second, there is no private property and no need for money or currency. Every citizen must turn over all of their possessions to a central storehouse. All of the goods a citizen requires are obtained at this same warehouse. Citizens are not paid for work, since all goods are given out freely at the storehouse. Utopia has no poverty; everyone has all of their needs met from the storehouse or other service centers.[36]

In Utopia, life is completely regimented. Everyone wears identical functional clothing. No personal adornments are permitted. Citizens, who become disabled or who are seriously ill, are encouraged to commit suicide. Suicide is seen as a humanitarian act because it alleviates the citizen's pain and suffering. Plus, it prevents the sick or elderly from becoming a burden on the perfect society.[37]

This Utopia, however, while wildly idealistic, ignores all the realities of constructing the perfect society in the real world. Of course, it violates human nature and circumvents human dignity. Nevertheless, impractical and unrealistic socialist academics and activists continue to try to create the perfect society found in *Utopia.*

Thomas Hobbes (Author of *Leviathan*) – Another Socialist Thinker

A third early socialist thinker was the philosopher Thomas Hobbs, who offered the world a somewhat conflicting set of socialist political concepts that he thought actually represented a new science of politics. Hobbes fashioned his new political science much in the same manner as Galileo, Harvey, and Descartes gave the world a profound new scientific revolution.[38]

His famed book *Leviathan* was first published in 1651 and described a political model for an absolute state.[39] It was a model in essence for a strong socialist or communist government.

While *Leviathan* was a word that conveyed the notion of a large sea monster, it was meant to be associated with a commonwealth or a state. In political parlance today, it generally refers to a totalitarian state.[40]

Why did his political ideas appear to contradict one another? His support for both strong political totalitarianism and human individuality at first seem difficult to reconcile.[41]

On the one hand, Thomas Hobbes proposed an absolute totalitarian model for nations with a powerful sovereign at its helm. His sovereign held monopoly power over all his subjects. In turn, the subjects only had freedom in limited areas that the sovereign might permit.[42]

Examples of the power of the sovereign include:

- Once a social contract is made between the sovereign and the subjects to form a commonwealth, the subjects cannot make a new social contact without the permission of the sovereign.
- Sovereign power cannot be forfeited. That means no individual in the social contract can ever be free from the social contract.
- The Sovereign exercises absolute control including control over the churches, the university curriculum, as well as what books and thoughts can be read and taught.
- No subject can protest against the Sovereign or the Institution of the Sovereign.
- No actions of the Sovereign can be punished by the subjects.
- The Sovereign is not subject to any laws.
- The Sovereign can judge all disputes, both civil and criminal.
- The Sovereign has the right to make all rules that the subjects must follow.[43]

On the other hand, Hobbes also believed in human individuality with all individuals sharing a common place in nature. Hobbes felt the all individuals existed in nature in an on-going state of war for survival. As such, he identified this as a type of equality, albeit an equality of fear and survival.[44]

To avoid the chaos of mankind trying to survive in nature in a constant state of war, as well as the associated confusion and uncertainty in their lives, individuals would enter into a social contract with a sovereign, who might be a totalitarian dictator or possibly a committee of shared leadership control[45] (such as a communist party, using the language of the 20th century).

To Hobbes, subjects would gladly relinquish their freedom and turn it over to the sovereign in order to obtain some sense of peace and security from the commonwealth that they did not have trying to survive on their own. The sovereign as the head of the Leviathan would have complete freedom over the subjects to provide their peace and security.[46]

Of course, this socialist thinking fails as did in our other examples because it shows no understanding of, or accommodation to, human dignity and human nature. But, some advocates of socialism probably used Hobbes thinking as a guidebook for designing socialist dictatorships.

Let's transition from the early socialist thinkers to actual attempts at implementing socialism or socialist thinking in the world.

The French Revolution and Socialism in the Late 1700s

Closely following the American Revolution in the late 1700s was the French Revolution that threw off the shackles of feudalism, ended the monarchy of King Louis XVI, and eventually ended in the Napoleonic Era.[47]

The French Revolution was largely triggered by the poor economic conditions existing at the time in France, along with the burden of heavy taxation. The Third Estate (ordinary citizens that were neither in the clergy nor in the aristocracy) sought more equal representation in the then Estates-General where the nobility held veto power over the so-called "commoners". Eventually, the Third Estate formed the National Assembly.[48]

Of course, the famous storming of the Bastille, the Reign of Terror, and the widespread bloodshed that followed are well known in history.[49]

But, what might not be as well-known is the part that socialist ideas and goals came into play in the terror, bloodshed, and violence in the French Revolution.[50]

While there were no socialist objectives specifically in mind during the storming of the Bastille, the main goal during the French Revolution was to promote the right of property. In the 1789 Declaration of the Rights of Man and Citizen, three rights were highlighted. These were the rights of "liberty, property, security" and they seemed very similar to America's 1776 Declaration of Independence and our rights of life, liberty, and the pursuit of happiness. The pursuit of happiness means, in effect, the right of property and the ability to use property for one's own life and enjoyment.[51]

To the original "liberty, property, security" rights, the French later added another right, equality. The problem for the French, however, was that it was no longer sufficient to simply end feudalism to obtain the goal of equality. Equality also required the elimination of private property (another intended right), and the creation of a new economic system to distribute property and wealth to obtain the utopian goal of equality among all citizens.[52]

The French champion of equality was Francois-Noel Babuef, who argued for socialist policies during the French Revolution. Babeuf (also known as Gracchus) believed that the equality he sought would result in abundance and it would allow citizens to work only a few hours per day at the job of their choice.[53] These were clearly socialist utopian ideas.

Just as in Sir Thomas More's *Utopia,* all the goods produced by citizens would be stored in a common store that also would be a central point of distribution of the goods back to the people, who subsequently needed them. Babeuf also thought money should be abolished and gold and silver should be forbidden as well. In the realm of education, Babeuf sought to create a same-sex national seminary for the indoctrination of all children in the ways of the new (socialist) system.[54]

During the French Revolution, socialist leaders hoped the principle of equality would become the religion of the land, replacing the Church. They sought to bring the Church under government control. In the process, hundreds of thousands of priests were killed and churches were closed down or ransacked all across the country. Even the Gregorian calendar based on the year of the birth of Christ was altered with Year 1 being the founding of the French Revolution.[55]

The French Revolution was permeated with an anti-Christian perspective and belief. It was a secular socialist country. It also represented a terribly violent and bloody attempt to impose socialism on a nation that originally sought liberty, security, and importantly at the time – property rights.

Ultimately, the French Revolution ended with General Napoleon Bonaparte taking control of the failed socialist French debacle in late 1799.

An American Experiment in Socialism in the Early 1800s

While Babeuf and others during the French Revolution sought to promote socialism with widespread terror, violence, and bloodshed, a British industrialist from Scotland named Robert Owen sought to develop a new humane social experiment in America. In sharp contrast to the public revolution in France, Owen believed that social change could be accomplished using the power of peaceful persuasion and private resources.[56]

Robert Owen's approach to socialism differed markedly from the early socialist thinkers Plato, More, and Hobbes and the French Revolution in that the power of government and government force and control were not necessary to create and maintain socialist communities. Whereas you might call the failed attempt at socialism in France to be "top-down socialism," the Owen idea might be better termed "bottom-up socialism."

It is interesting to note that although Babeuf pushed for his unnamed (socialist) revolution in France, Robert Owen and his followers actually coined the word "socialism" to describe Owen's "united social" system.[57]

Robert Owen was known as a humane businessman, who tried to improve the working conditions and lives of his employees.

For example, his cotton mill provided a good company store for workers to buys goods. His New Lanark mill was also known for its educational system where kindness to children was the norm.[58] Owen's paternalistic management style in many ways pre-dated 20th century American practices in some companies.

But, two principles surprisingly undergirded Owen's socialist philosophy. First, he believed that everyone was so influenced by others and their own background in life, that no one was responsible for their own will and actions. Second, Owen thought that it was ridiculous for men to think that they should be responsible to God and their fellow men for their own thoughts, wills, and actions. Owen was adamantly opposed to religion and wished he could eliminate religion from the world.[59]

Robert Owen also believed in the idea that a national plan for character formation could be put into place that would radically change people. His plan was an offshoot of his belief that human will and actions were imposed on people without their control. Owen wanted the State to require character formation.

In Owen's words:

> "That plan is a national, well-digested, unexclusive system for the formation of character ... the members of any community may by degrees be trained to live *without idleness, without poverty, without crime, and without punishment;* for each of these is the effect of error ..."[60]

Owen's first attempt at socialism in the United States was made near the Wabash River in Indiana. It was called New Harmony to signify its unified social nature. New Harmony failed despite Owen subsidizing it with $30,000 of his personal resources over and above the initial costs to get it started.[61]

On the 50th Anniversary on the Declaration of Independence, Owen delivered a bold speech that he thought would go down in posterity for its significance. He called it the Declaration of Mental Independence. Among his thoughts on July 4, 1826 were:

> "... man, up to this hour, has been, in all parts of the earth, a slave to a TRINITY of the most monstrous evils that could be combined to inflict mental and physical evil upon his whole race ... PRIVATE, OR INDIVIDUAL PROPERTY – ABSURD AND IRRATIONAL SYSTEMS OF RELIGION AND MARRIAGE ..."[62]

To Owen, marriage was simply "unnatural" and the cause of prostitution.[63]

Predictably, New Harmony failed for a number of reasons unforeseen by Owen. Some people rejected New Harmony's constitution due to its anti-religious tenor. But, human nature and basic economics resulted in further problems. Highly skilled workers were needed in some positions and they refused to come to New Harmony because of the low socialist wages offered. In addition, New Harmony was saddled with the burden of an overabundance of unskilled workers that produced little, yet whose needs were at least equivalent to average citizens. Besides labor and production challenges, New Harmony was beset with distribution issues as well.[64]

Despite several reorganizations, Owen's socialist experiment in America in the early 1800s failed dramatically. Notwithstanding Owen's optimism, grandiose public speaking, and personal fortune, the reality of socialism eventually kicked in and socialism fizzled again.

Socialism, Communism, Scientific Socialism, and Marxism – Marx and Engels

When one discusses socialism at any length, the name Karl Marx inevitably comes to mind rather quickly. Yet that off-hand association misses the significant fact that Friedrich Engels[65] was largely responsible for linking the name of Karl Marx to socialism and for promoting socialism widely over the years. Engels preferred taking a back seat to Marx's well known persona and for promoting socialism and communism in the background.[66]

Importantly, Engels also is known for writing the preliminary draft of *The Communist Manifesto*[67], while Marx penned the final draft.[68] Both names are listed as the authors of record.

Four distinct terms are linked to Karl Marx and Friedrich Engels – socialism, communism, scientific socialism, and Marxism. Some questions about these concepts immediately jump to mind.

What's the difference between the specific terms "socialism," and "communism," if any, that Karl Marx and Friedrich Engels used throughout their lives? Plus, are these two words still used in the same sense today?

Another question to consider: what do the labels "scientific socialism" and "Marxism" mean when discussing Marx and Engels? In fact, are there any differences at all among these four related terms?

Let's address these questions.

During their lives advocating communism, both Karl Marx and Friedrich Engels used the terms socialism and communism interchangeably. Once in 1875, Marx in discussing the German Democratic Party referenced a lower (or earlier) phase of a future communist society and a higher (or later) phase of an eventual communist society. Yet, he did not indicate the earlier phase was socialism and the later phase was communism. Neither Marx nor Engels differentiated between socialism and communism. They were equivalent concepts in their minds.[69]

What, then, did these synonymous terms mean to Karl Marx and Friedrich Engels?

In sharp contrast to the early utopian socialist thinkers that formulated models of the ideal social order, Marx and Engels developed a system of ideas that proposed the inevitability of communism. According to them, history indicates an economic progression or pattern of several developmental stages that go from feudalism, to capitalism, to socialism, and finally, to communism.

Scientific socialism was an attempt by Engels to bring his ideas together with those of Marx to explain their concept of communism's ultimate ascendency as the one and only global economic system.[70]

Note that they envisioned global communism as a global economic system only. They did not think it would ever become an international political system, because in their view political systems would no longer be needed under the ultimate economic system of communism. Political systems in their view were only needed in pre-communist systems, such as capitalism.[71]

Scientific socialism appeared in a book entitled *Anti-Duhring* and in a subsequent pamphlet called *Socialism: Utopian and Scientific* that contained excerpts from *Anti-Duhring*[72].

Here are the fundamental ideas that constitute scientific socialism and for that matter, Marx and Engels' socialism and communism as well:

- Historical materialism
- Class struggle
- Surplus value
- Contradictions of capitalism
- Dynamics of the business cycle
- Economic impoverishment
- Political rise of the proletariat
- Inevitable revolution
- Dying of the State
- Fulfillment of mankind as it ascends from "the kingdom of necessity to the kingdom of freedom"[73]

In this view, scientific socialism is the realization by Marx of the class struggle that existed throughout history – the bourgeois vs. the proletariat, or the capitalist vs. the workers, in more modern terminology.[74]

Materialism is a philosophical concept that the only thing that exists in life is matter. Atheism seems to follow directly from that thought and explains the fact that many materialists are also atheists.

Taking materialism one step further, historical materialism in the context of scientific socialism sees that the basis of all social structures revolves around the production needed to sustain human life (what is produced), the actual production (how it is produced), and the exchange of goods once produced (how it is distributed).[75]

Scientific socialism weaves together all these elements into a complex and convoluted explanation of why capitalism will fail, socialism will follow, and why communism is inevitable.

Moreover, despite its name, scientific socialism does not appear to offer any true scientific evidence that their claims are valid. In addition, their theories, hypotheses, and vague generalities are not based on solid empirical data that can be verified quantitatively.

Dense and muddled spaghetti-like diatribes in the writings of Marx and Engels certainly do little to convince many readers that scientific socialism makes any theoretical sense, let along practical sense.

Once again, socialism fails in theory. Historical materialism neglects God and the human dignity, individual freedom, and morality that manifest themselves in the spiritual side of men and women of faith. It also ignores the human nature men and women exhibit in their lives. Competition and motivation are common characteristics in men and women that can't be ignored.

Men and women have a spiritual dimension that is normally present in their lives. To create a social order that rejects that spiritual nature of mankind completely is destined to fail as we have seen in socialist nations and experiments over the years.

Finally, what is Marxism? Does it differ from socialism, communism, and scientific socialism? Simply put, Marxism is another term used to describe the work of Marx and Engels in general. It is essentially one more word to describe socialism and communism.

Let's look at one more subtle point about the use of the terms socialism and communism.

Evolutionary Socialism vs. Revolutionary Socialism

One protégé of Engels in the late 1890s, Eduard Bernstein, began examining actual empirical evidence related to capital accumulation, class struggles, and the improvement in the economic and social lives of workers in capitalist nations versus the vastly different expectations predicted by so-called scientific socialism.[76]

Bernstein uncovered what he believed were specific "Problems of Socialism" where the socialist theory of Marx and Engels were wrong and where it was contradictory. In 1899, Eduard Bernstein summed up his factually based criticism of scientific socialism in a book called *Empirical Socialism*. One of his basic thoughts was that communism could proceed from capitalism by means of social democracy, avoiding Marx and Engels' inevitable revolutionary approach.[77]

It turns out that in the 20th century, some other socialists differed from Marx and Engels in their use of the terms socialism and communism much like Bernstein. These socialists did distinguish between socialism and communism along the lines of the actual strategy and tactics used to achieve a future communist society.[78]

Socialists, who wanted to achieve socialism more slowly through democratic means by promotion and debate, retained the title socialists.[79] This became known to many as "evolutionary socialism." To these socialists, what they sought was called socialism.

On the other hand, those socialists, who wanted to bring about communism much more quickly through revolution, bloodshed, violence, riots, and civil war, were called communists.[80] In contrast to "evolutionary socialism," this was termed "revolutionary socialism" and their objective was clearly called communism.

This dichotomy of terms was a vast departure from the views of Karl Marx and Friedrich Engels in the 19th century that considered the words socialism and communism interchangeable. Of course, Marx and Engels' preferred strategy and tactics for socialism and communism that were revolutionary in nature and consistently involved both revolution and civil war as their path of choice to achieving communism.[81]

Marxism – An Irreconcilable Contradiction

If you think about the writings of Karl Marx and Friedrich Engels, they created an irreconcilable contradiction between their strategy and tactics for achieving communism, namely, revolution and civil war, and their socialist theory.[82] Why?

Recall that to them communism is inevitable. It follows in their socialist theory that capitalism must fail, socialism will replace it, and eventually communism will take the place of socialism. In other words, after capitalism will come communism and it will be inescapable.

But, if that were true, why did Marx need to develop revolutionary socialist parties committed to violence. According to well-known free market economist Ludwig von Mises: "Their aim was to rise in rebellion, to establish the dictatorship of the proletarians and to exterminate mercilessly all bourgeois."[83]

Certainly, Marx and Engels showed a major disconnect between their socialist theory of the inevitability of communism and their actions toward encouraging violence and bloodshed to bring about communism. If they believed that communism was truly inevitable, why was revolution and civil war a necessity in their world?

Next, let's turn our attention to several actual socialist efforts in the 20th century. We will see that socialism not only fails in theory, but it also fails in real world practice.

Chapter 3

What are Examples of Socialism from the 20th Century On?

The 20th century is replete with failed attempts at both evolutionary socialism and revolutionary socialism. At the peak of socialism's inroads into national politics in the 1980s, about 70 different countries could be called socialist. These can be further subdivided into three specific categories: communist, (third world) socialist, and social democracy countries.[84]

Here are a few examples from the 1980s.

- Communist countries included: U.S.S.R., China, East Germany, Czechoslovakia, Cambodia, North Korea, Nicaragua, Vietnam, and Yugoslavia.
- Among those that fall under the category of third world socialist nations were: Angola, Costa Rica, Zimbabwe, Sudan, Rwanda, PDR Yemen, Democratic Republic of Congo (Zaire), El Salvador, Seychelles, and Mozambique.
- Countries that might best be termed a social democracy included: France, Austria, Australia, Spain, Portugal, Greece, and New Zealand.[85]

With about 70 examples of socialism to choose from in the 20th century, there are no shortages of failed socialist and communist examples to consider. In this chapter, we will select a few countries to illustrate how socialism fails in the real world.

Let's start our 20th century tour of failed socialist countries by looking at the Russian Revolution and communism.

The Russian Revolution and Communism – Lenin and Stalin

While many students of history refer to 1917 as the year of the Russian Revolution, the implication that there was one Russian Revolution is not quite accurate. It is probably more factual to say that there were actually two Russian Revolutions in 1917 – one in February 1917 and the other in October 1917.[86]

To be even more precise, the February 1917 Russian Revolution might be termed a true political revolution, while the October 1917 Russian Revolution is better described as a coup d'état. While both led to the ultimate totalitarian communist regime under Lenin, they were distinctly different events in Russian history.[87]

Ironically, the Russian Revolution started out as an attack on the tsarist monarchy of Nicholas II in order to avert a revolution. At the time, many were tired with Russia's military record of attrition and simply wanted to avoid additional Russian military and political decline and also wanted to strengthen the government. Yet, opposition grew significantly enough during the period that the Russian generals convinced Tsar Nicholas II it was necessary to abdicate. With the abdication, the entire Russian government collapsed completely.[88]

This was the February 1917 Russian Revolution and it was followed quickly by the formation of a Provisional Government that had widespread acceptance nationally.[89]

In contrast, the October 1917 revolution was a coup d'état against the Provisional Government led by the Bolshevik Party. This was the political party that Lenin had personally founded and controlled. The coup d'état was orchestrated by a relatively small band of organizers close to Lenin, and initially began by trying to foment street demonstrations to bring down the existing Provisional Government. When this tactic failed, special shock troops were given the mission of seizing key government infrastructure targets. The coup d'état succeeded.[90]

Lenin gained totalitarian control not by any special oratorical skills or statesmanship, but rather by his military prowess. He had read the Prussian General Carl von Clausewitz's book *On War* that dealt with military strategy. Lenin then saw his political opponents much like military enemies, and he believed his enemies must be annihilated, not just subdued.[91]

Historian Richard Pipes further described Lenin with these words: "Lenin had a strong streak of cruelty. He condemned people to death by the thousands without remorse, though also without pleasure."[92]

In particular, Lenin was guided by something Marx said in 1871, commenting on the disintegration of the Paris Commune back in the days of the French Revolution. Retrospectively, Marx felt the Paris Commune failed because it made a fundamental error – it did not completely liquidate the then existing political, social, and military structures. It should not have allowed control to pass to new people.[93] Instead, it should have destroyed the old system first before building a new political and social order.

Lenin's personality according to one individual, who knew him fairly well, described Lenin's primary disposition as hateful. He certainly did not get along well with people and he could not tolerate any type of dissent. If you were not Lenin's friend, or you were not a member of his Bolshevik Party, or you disagreed with Lenin, you were classified as his enemy. Lenin's enemies had to be silenced in his rigid view.[94]

Lenin consolidated power and established a totalitarian communist country.

Bolsheviks then sought to export communism around the world, not satisfied with their power at home. They hoped to find nations that utilized private property and turn them into a worldwide union of socialist countries. Regime change on a global scale was their vision for totalitarian communism.[95]

In the economic sphere, Lenin thought his brand of brutal terror would result in a powerful economy in a short period of months. But, like other socialist nations, Lenin destroyed the economy he took over. Socialism failed miserably under totalitarian communism.[96]

Joseph Stalin followed Lenin as a ruthless and brutal communist dictator. He first popped up on Lenin's radar in the early 1900s before the Russian Revolution for his success in so-called expropriations. These expropriations consisted of bank robberies and armored car holdups (sometimes killing people caught up in the robberies) for the purpose of raising funds for the Bolshevik Party and Lenin's revolutionary activities.[97]

Later, to assure party unity and to enforce a ban on party factions that hurt the Bolshevik Party, Lenin created the new post of general secretary with Stalin selected to occupy the new role.[98] After a series of strokes and poor health, Lenin died and Stalin filled the communist dictator's position.[99]

The Red Terror, The Great Terror, and The Great Famine

Communism during and following the Russian Revolution took the lives of about 20 million people according to one source through executions, man-made famines and starvation, deportations that resulted in deaths during transit or confinement in tight spaces, and forced labor with subsequent deaths caused by exhaustion, hunger, medical issues, and extreme weather.[100]

The Red Terror, The Great Terror, The Great Famine, forced collectivization, forced dekulakization, concentration camps, and the Gulag System were all manifestations of the spiritual and moral depravity of this brand of socialism.[101]

Without question, this barbarous form of socialism implemented by Lenin and continued under Stalin traced its human suffering and misery back to the warped ideas of Marx and Engels.

Boris Yeltsin, head of Russia decades later, summed up the Russian Revolution and communism in a speech made before the U. S. Congress with these words:

> "The world can sigh in relief. The idol of Communism which spread everywhere social strife, animosity, and unparalleled brutality, which instilled fear in humanity, has collapsed. It has collapsed never to rise again."[102]

The Russian Revolution and communism are one monstrous example of a socialist failure in practice.

Let's turn to another horrific socialist failure, Nazism.

National Socialism (Nazism) in Germany – Hitler

Another bitter flavor of socialism in the 20th century was National Socialism or Nazism led by Hitler in Germany. While the socialism of Marx and Engels as well as the socialism of Lenin were internationally focused, the version of socialism led by the National Socialist German Worker's Party combined socialism with a highly charged form of nationalism.

Not everyone probably realizes that Nazism and fascism (covered in the next section) are both true variations of socialism, but they are. They are certainly not far right ideologies as some might suggest.

One reason, why many people have been misled over the years about Nazism and fascism being far right politically, is that there was a directed propaganda campaign launched by the Russian dictator Joseph Stalin following World War II to damage nations that believed in freedom and free markets with the far right fascist label.[103]

That disinformation campaign equated capitalism with fascism. Of course, socialists often deceive people in their efforts to achieve their dual objectives of power and control of nations.[104]

It is important to realize too what has largely been lost over the decades. The Nazi rise to power in Germany happened as the Nazi movement fought for and campaigned for socialism for Germany.[105]

Even the Nazi flag was significant in its design. It included: "... a black swastika inside a white disk in a sea of red." It was intended to attract communists to their cause. The red color symbolized socialism, the white color was a token of nationalism, and the swastika was a pattern used to represent their perceived Aryan struggle.[106]

At the heart of National Socialism was an intense and virulent set of beliefs that attacked capitalism. Nazism was adamantly opposed to individual profits, banks, and international finance.[107]

National Socialism did permit some private property ownership along with some private business ownership, certainly more than in the Soviet Union. But, Nazism chose to regulate such private businesses extensively. In addition,

National Socialism also decided to nationalize some industries as well permitting some private businesses.[108]

In terms of education, Nazism believed that the government should indoctrinate all German children in socialist academics at government expense.[109]

One interesting contradiction in Hitler's expressed socialist philosophy dealt with Marxism. On the one hand, he acknowledged how his National Socialism was built on the ideas of Marx. But, on the other hand, he also indicated he wanted to destroy Marxism.[110]

Possible reasons for the contradiction include his fiercely anti-Jewish thinking and the fact that Karl Marx was of Jewish heritage and that tainted Marx's work in Hitler's view. Another reason might be that Marxism was focused on international socialism, while Hitler was a vehement national socialist.[111]

Not only was Nazism strongly opposed to capitalism, and favored the usual tenets of socialism, such as wielding total control from a centralized government, no tolerance for those that dispute their views, and indoctrination of school children,[112] National Socialism was also responsible for millions of deaths.

Most citizens are familiar with the genocide of six million Jews killed by the Nazis during the horrific Holocaust. But, the death toll under National Socialism was even more staggering.[113]

According to political scientist and social science researcher, R. J. Rummel, at the University of Hawaii, "the Nazis murdered … most likely closer to 21 million men, women, handicapped, aged, sick, prisoners of war, forced laborers, camp inmates, critics, homosexuals, Jews, Slavs, Serbs, Czechs …" and others. Brutally, included in this death toll were over 1,000,000 children under the age of 18 years old.[114]

Despite some private businesses (that were highly regulated and controlled), the Nazi economy morphed from capitalism to socialism with the usual problems a socialist economy faces. Overall, National Socialism failed the German people.

Clearly, National Socialism under Hitler was another appalling and gruesome, failed socialist government.

Let's look at another version of socialism that focused on nationalism, not international socialism.

National Fascist Party in Italy – Mussolini

Fascism in Italy looked much like Nazism in Germany. It was nationally focused versus other socialists who sought to extend their ideology internationally. Much like National Socialism in Germany, it permitted some private enterprises while nationalizing other industries. Private businesses were extensively controlled and regulated in the best interests of the State, or at least what the government deemed to be in the best interest of the State.[115]

In this case, it was led by Benito Mussolini, a somewhat enigmatic leader that oversaw a cult of followers. He was termed *Il Duce* which meant the commander. His governing philosophy seemed to evolve over time, as pragmatic considerations emerged – from anarchism to socialism, to international socialism, to national socialism.[116] Like Hitler, Mussolini converged on the Italian version of Germany's National Socialism. But, it was nevertheless distinct and different from the German version.

For example, in an attempt to make Italy great, Mussolini promoted population growth in some curious and noteworthy ways. He encouraged large families, he prohibited birth control, and he stopped emigration. But, in addition, Mussolini also added a novel socialist twist; he initiated a special tax on "unjustified celibacy."[117]

Mussolini was an avowed atheist, who went so far as to say that having religious faith was truly a mental illness in need of psychiatric attention.[118]

At a socialist conference early in his public life, Mussolini also promoted a resolution that stated Catholicism or any other mainstream monotheistic religion was incompatible with socialism. Further, any socialists, who practiced their faith or who allowed their children to practice their faith, should be expelled from the socialist party. Mussolini also insisted that socialists in the party reject religious marriage, Baptism, and other Christian ceremonies.[119]

Another major aspect of Mussolini's life was his claimed sexual prowess. He touted having 169 mistresses over his active sexual lifetime, starting his sexual exploits at the young age of 17 with a prostitute. He even cultivated the odd persona of being every Italian woman's marriage partner.[120]

What was the economic track record during fascism? Just like other socialist nightmares, fascism under Italian National Socialism was a dismal failure. The heavy regulations, the centralized planning, the micromanagement of the economy, and the extensive bailouts of favored industries all assured a poor overall economic performance. Taxpayers, of course, paid a hefty bill in Italy for these failed socialist policies.[121]

With that look at the failed socialist attempts at governing through Nazism and fascism, let's view a completely different manner of implementing socialism.

Kibbutzim Socialist Communities and the Jewish Resettlement in Palestine

Prior to the Jewish resettlement in Palestine and Israel's War of Independence (1948 – 1949), the first kibbutz, Deganya, was started around 1910.[122] By 1940, over 80 kibbutzim had been formed with a total population of nearly 27,000 members in the region.[123]

What were the actual kibbutzim socialist communities like in practice? According to Joshua Muravchik, foreign policy expert and author:

> "The kibbutzim practiced socialism of a very pure kind. The members rotated jobs, took their meals in a common dining hall, lived in identical little dwellings and deposited their offspring while still in swaddling clothes in children's homes. The youngsters lived and studied with their peers, save for a few hours' visit with parents each evening."[124]

Each kibbutz had roughly several hundred members and the early kibbutzim focused primarily on agricultural products such as bananas, grapes, olives, corn, and soybeans as well as fishing. Later, kibbutzim added other products and services including: a plastics factory, medical appliances, tourism, a guesthouse, and a restaurant. At its peak in the middle of the 20th century, the sum of all kibbutzim reached a total population of about 130,000 inhabitants.[125]

Some socialists gushed over the early accomplishments of the kibbutzim for living such a model version of idealistic socialism. For example, after the fall of the Soviet Union, Gorbachev decided to visit kibbutz Ein Gedi and raved "this is what we meant by socialism."[126] Of course, in stark contrast, Lenin and Stalin killed millions of innocent citizens to achieve their version of socialism, while the kibbutzim strictly relied on peaceful means to develop their kibbutzim socialist communities.

Despite its peaceful and modestly productive early beginnings, how did the kibbutzim fare in the long run? The quick answer is that the kibbutzim concept failed for a number of basic reasons.

For one thing, the heyday of the kibbutzim lasted only one generation. The first generation of kibbutzim inhabitants were fired up about the idea of community sharing and the arguments for socialist equality. By the second generation, the children of the initial founders of the kibbutzim were less inclined to follow their parent's lifestyle preferences. Then, with the third generation, came a real desire for change. The perceived benefits the first generation saw in a socialist community no longer appealed to the third generation, and many sought a more typical lifestyle, such as that capitalism generally offers citizens.[127]

Another basic reason for the decline in the popularity of the kibbutzim was financial. The government of Israel was generous in its tax breaks, subsidies, and contracts to the kibbutzim for many years. When Menachem Begin a conservative was elected Prime Minister in 1977, the State of Israel pulled back on its financial support for the kibbutzim. This was an added strain on the kibbutzim socialist communities.[128]

In addition to these factors, human nature played a part in the kibbutzim's downturn. Some workers with premium skills could obtain better incomes working in traditional jobs away from the kibbutzim. Higher salaries and wages acted as a financial incentive that was difficult to overcome by the kibbutzim. Plus, lower skilled workers were drawn to the benefits the kibbutzim offered them. In the minds of many top flight workers, they felt they deserved to be paid at higher market levels, not the mere subsistence levels they would get in the kibbutzim.[129]

One kibbutz Ginosar member captured the negative sentiment of some kibbutzim inhabitants discussing those who avoided work calling the kibbutz a "paradise for parasites."[130]

The kibbutzim worked for a while on a limited small town scale, certainly not at the level of an entire country. But, it ultimately was not self-sustaining in a financial sense. It heavily relied on a capitalist economy for funding. The State of Israel lavished the kibbutzim with considerable government contracts, tax breaks, and subsidies. Without the infusion of funding by a capitalist market economy, it would likely have failed more dramatically.

Similar to the Scandinavian Socialism we looked at earlier, the kibbutzim socialist communities were small welfare-subsidized communities funded by capitalism.

Let's next turn our attention to the Chinese version of socialism which has morphed over the years, but still remains a communist country with significantly curtailed freedom.

Chinese Communism and Market Socialism – Mao and Deng

Mao Zedong (sometimes written Mao Tse-tung in some publications) declared the existence of the People's Republic of China (PRC) on October 1, 1949. Mao's Chinese Communism was the outcome of a decade's long military struggle for power and control among three different groups of combatants.[131]

First, there were the local warlords, who controlled some regions of China as virtually independent smaller countries. Second, there were the nationalists, or the Kuomintang Party, led originally by Sun Yat-sen and later after Sun Yat-sen's death by Chiang Kai-shek. The nationalists sought national unity, self-determination, and democracy. They were also strongly anti-communist and were against Japan and its vision of uniting Asia under Japanese control. The third and final combatant in the struggle for power in China was the revolutionary communists under the Chinese Communist Party and its leader Mao Zedong.[132]

The communists prevailed among the three groups and gained control of mainline China. Chiang Kai-shek was relegated to Taiwan as China's opposition in exile. What was socialism like in the People's Republic of China?

Socialism in China was similar to communism in the Soviet Union, since the Chinese Communist party followed the same model of communism as in the Soviet Union. The soviets went so far as to supply the Chinese with advisors, including some that helped set up their own gulag.[133]

Mao completely replaced the traditional Chinese political and social system with a socialist dictatorship of the proletariat. The ideas put in place were those of Marx and Lenin from Mao's perspective and interpretation.

Most notable of the socialism followed by Mao was the brutal and horrific treatment of Chinese citizens. Prior to the creation of the PRC, the communists killed about 3,500,000 people. That's a conservative estimate made by political scientist and social science researcher, R. J. Rummel, at the University of Hawaii. He also indicates the precise number of citizens murdered by the communists before the creation of the PRC in October 1949 might range up to 11,700,000. Obviously, clear-cut statistics are not easily found and data has to be pieced together with painstaking efforts.[134]

As terrible as the death total that was carried out by the communists to achieve power in China, the total death toll from 1949 through 1987 under the communists is conservatively estimated to be 35,200,000. Of this total, 27,000,000 citizens starved to death as a result of the "Great Leap Forward" collectivization of the peasants that essentially destroyed the Chinese agricultural system. This is the worst known recorded famine in the history of civilization.[135]

The forced socialism thrust on the Chinese people was an incredibly bloody and deadly socialist experiment that failed miserably, yielding unbelievable human heartache, suffering, and tragedy.

Another thought to be reliable source of death statistics published by Harvard University Press, estimates the human death toll associated with Chinese Communism to be 65,000,000 citizens killed. So, the conservative estimates stated above for Chinese citizens killed under socialism might actually be on the low side.[136]

With regard to China's economy, despite all the so-called socialist and communist reforms from 1949 through 1978, the average Chinese citizen lived on a substance of about one dollar per day, certainly not even in the ballpark with nations living under free market or capitalist systems.[137]

With Deng Xiaoping's ascendency to the top post in China, Deng flirted with some market reforms to attempt to bolster China's paltry economic output. He alternated with allowing some economic and political freedom and then reneging on those same reforms.[138] During the economic reforms and in particular as a result of one specific reform, the household responsibility system, the economic growth rate grew to about 12% per year for a decade. The household responsibility system, a Deng program, consisted of giving individuals, families, or small teams modest parcels of land to farm by themselves. The proceeds of their farming efforts could be distributed freely as they saw fit, after a small tax or share of the crops were paid to the State.[139]

This micro-capitalist idea worked astonishingly well in stark contrast to the decades of failed Chinese agricultural so-called "reforms."

Deng dubbed his capitalist efforts as "socialism with Chinese characteristics" or a "socialist market economy."[140] Some term this type of approach as "market socialism." This is essentially a socialist political system with some market flexibility added in to gain economic growth. Usually, such systems still deny citizens basic human freedoms.

The bottom line is simple. Socialism, including its communist variations, always leads on a path to spiritual, moral, and economic bankruptcy. The results are a poverty-stricken economy, and in many instances, with millions and millions of its people tortured and murdered for an ideology that never works, without help from capitalism.

When will people around the world wake up to real world socialism and its devastation on citizens?

Let's turn our attention to two more examples of real world socialism in the 20th century – both took place in Great Britain.

British Labour Party, Social Democracy, and Democratic Socialism – Attlee

Socialism came to Great Britain twice in the 20th century and in both cases, it was much different than with Chinese Communism. There was neither the bloodshed nor the violence that took place in China under communism. But, in both instances in Great Britain, socialism did result in economic disappointment and financial decline.[141]

Early in the 20th century, the center of socialist discussion in Great Britain seemed to be the Fabian Society whose membership included a group of notable individuals such as Bertrand Russell, George Bernard Shaw, and H. G. Wells.[142]

The Fabian Society clearly rejected the Marxist socialist principles of class struggle, historical materialism, revolution, and the inevitability of communism as the end state of global governance. Their objective was complete socialism, even though the Fabian Society tried to promote total socialism in an evolutionary manner and not through revolution, violence, or civil war.[143]

The Independent Labour Party (ILP) was also established in Britain and advocated a strong platform centered on socialism. When the subsequent Labour Party (LP) was formed by the Trades Union Congress and then merged with the ILP, the British Labour party became the home of those pushing socialism in Great Britain.[144]

Of particular significance was the well-known Clause IV in the Labour Party's Constitution that cemented the socialist ideology they chose to pursue. In part Clause IV stated that:

"... to secure for the producers by hand and brain the full fruits of their industry, and the most equitable distribution thereof that may be possible, upon the basis of the common ownership of the means of production and the best obtainable system of public administration and control of each industry or service."[145]

Clearly, the common ownership of the means of production was an essential component of socialism in general, and Marxism in particular. In the United Kingdom, it translated into the British Labour Party's support for the widespread nationalization of industries.

A prominent member of the Labour Party was Clement Attlee. His public life included work as a volunteer, soldier, and politician. In Attlee's view, his most satisfying effort was supporting Winston Churchill during World War II. Clement Attlee, in fact, helped form the coalition government under Churchill. He also played a pivotal role in the War Cabinet, consisting of Churchill, Attlee, Chamberlain, Halifax, and Greenwood.[146]

Though it took years, the leader of the Labour Party, Clement Attlee eventually became Prime Minister in 1945 promising a peace dividend following the arduous efforts of the Brits in World War II. Attlee's desired socialism was finally given a chance in Great Britain.[147]

Top on the list of socialist changes led by Attlee was the nationalization of key industries throughout Great Britain. The Bank of England and the coal mining industry started off the

road to British socialism. Other industries followed quickly –
trucking, railroads, communications, civil aviation, gas and
electricity.[148]

The welfare state, replete with numerous programs,
accompanied the efforts surrounding nationalizations.
Examples of the new welfare programs were: free health care
coverage, unemployment insurance, retirement coverage,
death benefits, and some public housing construction.
Additionally, the Attlee government chose to discourage
private housing construction, despite the considerable
number of homes that the private sector could have provided
to the citizens of Great Britain.[149]

Understandably, Attlee's efforts were met with criticism from
former Prime Minister Winston Churchill and other
conservatives. They felt the Attlee government was not
meeting the short-term, post war needs of the British people
by devoting so much effort to long-term projects, such as the
nationalization of key industries. The immediate needs of the
people were "food, homes and work." Nationalizations were
both a policy distraction and a resource sink at a time that the
Attlee government faced bankruptcy.[150]

To Attlee's opponents, his government's efforts were
motivated and "impelled by Socialist theory."[151]

What happened to the British economy next? How did it fare
under socialism? Plus, who paid the bill for all the new
welfare programs?

It turned out that several industries needed government
subsidies to keep their products and services flowing.

Shortages developed. Attlee even had to resort to rationing a basic commodity, bread. The economy languished first and then declined precipitously. Ultimately, capitalism came to Great Britain's assistance in the form of the American Marshall Plan, which gave the government of Great Britain a loan of $3.75 billion.[152]

Once more, capitalism bailed out a failed socialist welfare state, this time in Great Britain under the leadership pf Prime Minister Clement Attlee.

Despite the Marshall Plan aid, the socialist government's monetary policy of easy money caused considerable inflation that resulted in even more headaches for the British economy. Finally, the Attlee government had to retrench and pullback from its expansive and expensive welfare state trajectory. Not surprisingly, the Labour party was voted out of office and the Conservatives regained control of the British Parliament.[153]

British Labor Party, Designer Socialism, and Christian Socialism – Blair

Despite Attlee's foray into "Social Democracy" or "Democratic Socialism," Great Britain would try once again late in the 20th century to make socialism a viable political and economic system. This time the leader of the British Labour Party was Tony Blair.[154]

Tony Blair sought to finally obtain a Labour Party victory after a string of losses to the Conservative Party. His method, and indeed his platform for the Labour Party surprised, and in some cases, shocked many socialists. Indeed, Tony Blair's

New Labour program appeared to be a Conservative Party's talking points agenda.[155]

Some critics renamed Tony Blair as "Tony Blur" because he appeared to be blurring the long held principles of socialism. Others called his form of socialism "Designer Socialism" because he picked only some socialist beliefs and added them to other conservative principles, fashioning a unique tapestry of political points.[156]

Because Tony Blair was personally a religious person, some citizens went so far as to call his New Labour "Christian Socialism." But, if it were meant to be a Christian version of socialism, it must have abandoned many components of Marxism that the atheist Karl Marx argued adamantly for, and wanted followers to embrace and adopt.[157]

In fact, Christian Socialism is a misleading phrase that might seduce some Christians into supporting socialism.[158]

Based on what socialism meant originally and how it has usually been implemented around the world, "Christian Socialism" is a contradiction in terms. Christian faith stands in direct conflict with atheism and the corresponding moral vacuum associated with socialism.

Let's next look at some other features in the blurry cloud of Designer Socialism.

Consider a New Labour plank in Tony Blair's Designer Socialism platform. The British Labour Party endorsed privatization (over its previous policy position of nationalization of British industries). Blair also stated what easily could be mistaken for a conservative policy assessment, namely, that "the era of tax and spend is dead and buried." Surprisingly, the Labour Party went so far as to rewrite Clause IV in their Constitution that had lasted nearly a century. Now, in their Constitution, New Labour actually supported "a thriving private sector," rather than a powerful public sector.[159]

Making changes to Clause IV was both a dramatic revision to the Labour Party's Constitution and an ideological revolution in their socialist thinking. Why did Tony Blair propose and endorse such a sea change transformation?

In developing the New Labour program, Tony Blair recognized some vital insights into the political and economic climate of the United Kingdom in the late 20th century. First, he believed that both the State and the public sector could grow so cumbersome and unwieldy that they work against the best interests of citizens. Second, Blair also perceived that the public didn't necessarily want the State making life decisions for them, even if citizens are better educated or more prosperous than in past decades.[160]

Indeed, Tony Blair might have missed the salient fact that freedom is a human right derived from our human dignity as children of God. It is also the self-evident desire of all people – educated or not, affluent or not. Freedom is not simply for the elite.

Tony Blair became Prime Minister of the United Kingdom in 1997 with a version of socialism that sounded more like capitalism – in essence, an ideological victory for capitalism, freedom, and free markets.

To repeat Oscar Wilde in his popular line:

> "Imitation is the sincerest form of flattery that mediocrity can pay to greatness."[161]

Tony Blair's need to sound like a capitalist in order to win an election for the long-time socialist British Labour Party is a telling story.

One unusual wrinkle in Prime Minister Tony Blair's capitalist-sounding Designer Socialism was that he allowed Gordon Brown to be the Chancellor of the Exchequer, during his time as Prime Minister. While Gordon Brown was a leading figure in the Labour Party, Brown was nevertheless not aligned completely with Blair's political rhetoric.[162]

Instead, Gordon Brown lavishly borrowed and spent money on various welfare projects in an attempt to boost popularity among the electorate. Tony Blair did not override those questionable financial decisions. In fact, United Kingdom's indebtedness rose from £323 Billion to a staggering £617 Billion, nearly doubling the debt in a relatively short period of time.[163]

Socialism failed to catch fire and win the long-range approval of citizens in the United Kingdom twice in the 20th century. Plus, its impact on the British economy was mixed. Once again, socialism failed in practice to achieve its pretentious economic goals. But, fortunately for Great Britain, capitalism bailed out the mistakes of Designer Socialism.

With that look at real world examples of socialism prior to the 20th century and during the 20th century, let's answer the question: why we are seeing a sudden rise in interest in socialism in America in the 21st century?

Chapter 4

What Caused the Sudden Rise of Interest in Socialism in America in the 21st Century?

It might seem like socialism has suddenly risen to a prominent role in American politics, culture, and discussion today. But, like a cold virus, it has been lurking in the shadows of our body politic, waiting for our immune political system to get tired and let it get a foothold. Then, in a moment of weakness, we feel a scratchy throat and soon thereafter a congested nose. In a day, we are overwhelmed with an upper respiratory infection that causes us misery —watery eyes and nose, sneezing, nasal congestion, coughing, phlegm, and fatigue.

Like the insidious cold virus mentioned above, socialism has been lurking in the political shadows of America's institutions, waiting to pounce on our Constitutional Republic and wreak havoc on our freedom and prosperity in a moment of forgetfulness or weakness or lack of education.

In fact, socialism unquestionably has been stealthily sneaking into our nation's institutions for decades, and actually has been covertly creeping into American's day-to-day lives for years. In some places, it has been unsuccessful. Yet, in other places, it has spread its utopian and unrealistic message.

But, recently it has been emboldened and has taken its deceitful message into the public square, counting on older generations of Americans to have largely forgotten socialism's consistent track record of spiritual, moral, political, and economic failure.

Indeed, many Americans forget the millions of victims of Soviet and Chinese socialism and communism. More recently, many don't even realize the suffering forced upon the Venezuelan people by democratic socialism that morphed into totalitarian dictatorship when socialist policies failed to live up to its promises and the people went without food and other necessities.

In parallel, socialists are also expecting the current generation of millennials to have little knowledge of our Founding Fathers' principles, the Constitution and the Rule of Law, as well as only a meager economic understanding of the overwhelming success of capitalism, individual freedom, morality, and free markets in the history of America.

On top of these reasons, socialists are also anticipating that America's younger generations have been indoctrinated with the deceitful message of socialist rhetoric in many K-12, and universities and colleges throughout America.

Now, let's turn to some of America's institutions that have been approached or infiltrated directly with socialist thinking.

Socialism Initially Rejected by the American Labor Movement

In both the 19th and 20th centuries, while the influence of Karl Marx and others sought to organize workers in Europe with socialism and communism, socialists in America unsuccessfully attempted to gain a foothold in the American labor union movement.[164]

Socialism was initially stopped in its tracks in America by its vehemently anti-communist labor leaders, such as Samuel Gompers and George Meany, who were adamantly opposed to communism and inherently suspicious of government control of labor.[165]

A subtle, yet profound, difference between the labor movements in Europe and America was found in those responsible for pushing socialism among the workers. In Europe, socialism was the darling of the privileged classes and intellectuals. They thrust it on workers thinking they knew what was best for the workers, who in turn never sought out or desired socialism. In contrast, in America, workers were organized and led by other workers. American labor leaders were not the product of the well-off, but rather typically came to be in power by rising from the ranks of the workers themselves.[166]

Samuel Gompers, for example, was an apprentice first to a shoemaker, and then became an apprentice in his father's cigar-making trade. Likewise, George Meany started as a plumber, again following in his father's footsteps. Both started out as workers and ended up as leaders in the American labor movement. Both were opposed to socialism, government control, and the idea of intellectuals telling workers how to run their unions.[167]

To highlight Samuel Gompers brightline patriotism, consider that after collapsing at a labor conference, his last words before dying were: "God bless our American institutions. May they grow better day by day."[168]

George Meany continued his vehement anti-communism throughout the 20th century, until his eventual retirement in 1979. His successor, Lane Kirkland, maintained a similar agenda. For example, with the assistance of the AFL-CIO's Longshoremen's union president, Thomas Gleason, and others, Kirkland supported workers in Poland, their trade union Solidarity, their efforts to end communist repression, and indirectly the complete end of the totalitarian dictatorship in Poland.[169]

Socialism Later Accepted by Some in the American Labor Movement

While the American labor movement consistently rejected socialism in all its variety of forms for decades, others in organized labor in the late 20th century succumbed to the seduction of socialist rhetoric. Some leaders have chosen to support left wing political causes and socialist progressive organizations.[170]

Not surprisingly, about 49% of American union members today are government workers. If these 7.16 million union members support both bigger socialist government programs as well as greater spending on salaries and wages, many people might understand their attempts to garner financial gains.[171]

But, while a small percentage of workers might see elusive pay increases as a result of socialism, their buying power will likely erode under the economic stagnation and decline that normally comes with socialism. It goes without saying those same government union workers would also feel their freedoms curtailed under socialist policies and programs.

Others in America have also been seduced by spurious socialist arguments. Take, for example, many American K – 12 public schools, universities and colleges.

Socialism Accepted and Promoted by Many in American K – 12 Public Schools, Universities and Colleges

It is probably clear to most objective observers that America's educational system from K-12, up to and including universities and colleges, is ideologically dominated by the Left.

It not only largely ignores the myriad of benefits and achievements that capitalism, freedom, and free markets have consistently produced in America, but it also openly accepts and promotes socialism. Additionally, it overlooks the fact that socialism is often a gateway to economic misery, famine, torture, murder, and totalitarian dictatorship.

Let's put some numbers on the Left's ideological power and influence on American college campuses. One study by a Brooklyn College professor found that among over 8,600 tenure-track professors in liberal arts colleges in America, registered Democrats exceeded registered Republicans by over 10 to 1.[172] That's an incredibly monolithic bias toward the Left and socialist thinking.

Young children in K-12 face similar lopsided socialist thought. One national survey completed by the Education Week Research Center found that only 27% of school teachers were Republicans. In addition, socialist causes and ideas show up throughout much of the K-12 public school system.[173] Consider some examples.

According to Justin Haskins, an executive editor and research fellow at The Heartland Institute:

> "From their earliest days, young students are taught by modern state curriculum standards to be cogs in the societal wheel rather than independent thinkers. The educational focus is often placed on performing well on standardized tests and memorizing facts, not learning how to make difficult moral choices or cogent arguments with classmates. Young children are constantly told "sharing is caring," and students routinely "earn" participation trophies for merely showing up."[174]

Another example is the grading system used in some schools. Students in these schools are not required to earn their grades. Many schools feel that poorly performing students will have their feelings hurt if they are given a bad grade. Still another challenge facing public school students can be open hostility toward conservative ideas.[175]

Examples abound, but the bottom line is clear. While America's founding moral principles and stellar economic growth and performance are downplayed, criticized, or ignored, the failed track record of socialism is hyped and overplayed.

Indoctrination is rampant in America's educational system and that fact has helped to empower today's socialists to openly promote socialism in America.

Besides support for socialism in the modern American labor movement and in American education, a large number of mainstream media outlets carry a Leftist outlook.

Socialism Often Promoted by the Mainstream Media

Just like the fact that American K – 12 public schools, universities and colleges appear to be dominated by socialist ideology, it's also true that the mainstream media – including most of the broadcast and cable TV media and most of the big city newspaper media – seem to be heavily influenced and controlled by both a socialist ideology and corresponding agenda.

It has even been suggested that the rise in "fake news" stories, news stories that later turn out to be untrue, can primarily be attributed to the socialist ideological bias of the mainstream media.[176]

Looking for a moment at just a subset of the mainstream media, financial journalists from a variety of publications including *The New York Times, The Washington Post, The Wall*

Street Journal, and the Associated Press, a research study done by Arizona State University and Texas A&M University learned that there were only about 4% of the journalists, who called themselves conservative. It's worth noting that financial journalists might be considered more likely to be conservative and to favor capitalism, freedom, and free markets, since they cover topics dealing with markets and capitalism in their everyday work.[177]

A Pew Research Center study took a different tack in attempting to explain bias in the media. They found that the "pervasive anti-"flyover state" bias that ignores the values of conservative Americans from the South and Midwest" can be attributed to the fact that about 22% of newsroom employees – including reporters, editor, and videographers, for example – live in just the three metro areas of New York, Washington, DC, and Los Angeles.[178]

Additionally, a significant proportion of newsroom employees, 41%, who support the internet publishing industry, also live in the Northeast.[179]

It's reasonable to assume values and viewpoints are related to geographical location. An observer need only review the 2016 presidential election map by red and blue colors, by counties, to see the dramatic differences between the vast array of red counties spanning large areas of the continental United States versus the relatively few blue counties found along the East and West coasts.

A few examples of how the media asserts Leftist or socialist thinking into their so-called news stories might shed further light on their influence on America.

To illustrate, consider the news stories when former New York City Mayor Michael Bloomberg threw out the possibility he might enter the presidential election race as a Democratic candidate. Here are some excerpts:

- "A potential shakeup in the race for president. Tonight, former New York City Mayor Michael Bloomberg. Is he about to run" [was it really a potential shakeup or is that exaggerating the story?] according to ABC anchor David Muir
- "sending a jolt through the presidential race" [without supporting evidence for the claim] stated ABC senior congressional correspondent Mary Bruce
- "a centrist who has become an active proponent of gun reform" [although some might claim Bloomberg sought extensive gun control] stated ABC senior congressional correspondent Mary Bruce[180]

In this case, it appeared that ABC was excited that Bloomberg entered the presidential race and was giving favorable media coverage.

In a second example of apparent Leftist and socialist bias, *NBC Nightly News* started a new series in the late fall of 2019. The new series, called "What Matters" interviewed Democratic voters attempting to give their ideas to Democratic presidential contenders. Not surprisingly, they didn't seem to care about what matters to Republican voters or to Republican candidates for office.[181]

Still another example shows how bogus a fake news story in the media can be in their day-to-day reporting. CNN reported in early November 2019 that "11,000 scientists warn of 'untold suffering' caused by climate change."[182] NBC News also issued a similar story based on the same warning in these words: "More than 11,000 scientists issue fresh warning: Earth faces a climate emergency."[183]

These certainly sound like legitimate stories supporting the socialist climate change meme. But, the problem is that they are not real news.

According to the Power Line website on November 8, 2019, "NBC News ... described a "study" produced by an "international consortium of more than 11,000 scientists." In reality, it turns out that there was no study and there weren't 11,000 scientists who delivered the warning. Instead, it was a press release and 11,000 people, who put their names on a webpage.[184]

Besides the impact of the mainstream media and their fake news stories and socialist themes on the current interest in socialism, socialism is also often promoted by the social media and their apparent Leftist bias.

Socialism Often Promoted by the Social Media and the High Tech Industry

Indeed, social media is a vital component of current communications in America and around the world. It's stunning to realize that Facebook and Twitter reach approximately 2 billion users with about 70% of Americans on Facebook. Unfortunately, there is evidence (anecdotally and intuitively as well as from more rigorous research) that social media might be playing ideological favorites, with Leftist and socialist thinking, people, and causes being favored and with conservatives being downplayed, dismissed, censored, or even banned completely.[185]

MRC NewsBusters captures the issue succinctly:

> "It's the new battleground of media bias. But it's worse. That bias is not a war of ideas. It's a war against ideas. It's a clear effort to censor the conservative worldview from the public conversation."[186]

Plus, a war against ideas is a clear violation of the spirit and letter of our First Amendment Constitutional guarantee of Freedom of Speech. It is a totalitarian mindset to censor and ban ideas that they disagree with in principle or practice.

The Media Research Center offers some findings on this type of behavior from Twitter, Facebook, Google, and YouTube:

- Twitter Shadow Banning – evidence of "shadow banning" by Twitter employees where conservatives are censored – simply put, some conservative tweets appear to be handled normally, but apparently their tweets are not distributed to followers
- Facebook Hiding Conservative Topics by Altering Trending Results – Some conservative topics are simply blacklisted. Examples include Sen. Rand Paul and the Conservative Political Action Conference

- Facebook Promoting Leftist Topics – Example: "Black Lives Matter" topic was promoted to trending results when the topic didn't numerically warrant such promotion
- Google Provided Biased Search Results for Clinton and the Democrats in the 2016 Election – One study found 2016 Google search results favored Clinton, while another study by Slate indicated Google search results favored both Clinton and other Democratic candidates. Google company chairman (as well as YouTube's chairman) Eric Schmidt was also involved in assisting the Clinton presidential campaign
- YouTube Shut Down Conservative Videos by Mistake or For Promoting Right-Wing Causes – YouTube has even touted its progressive attitudes and its support for Leftist causes[187]

Other means for promoting socialist thinking by social media is the use of Leftwing (so-called) fact-checkers that appear to support socialism and socialist causes. Their purported reason for existence is to eliminate fake news stories. But, how does using Leftists to curate news stories eliminate fake news stories (written by other Leftists, if the stories are fake to start with)? Any programs that use such fact-checkers are not in a position to provide ideological balance to a social media platform.[188]

Similar advisory groups suffer from the same deficiency. Twitter, for example, has 25 members in its Trust and Safety Council. Of the 25 member advisors, conservatives are outnumbered 12 to 1. There is definitely an issue with even-handed fairness and objectivity when getting such lopsided advice.[189]

To indicate how preposterous and nonsensical the consequence of banning conservative thinkers and conservative ideas from social media is in reality, just think about this point of view. Social media like Facebook, Twitter, Google, and YouTube are, in essence, public utilities much like a phone, gas, or electric company. In much the same manner as other utilities, they are needed and used by nearly everyone in the entire population.

Can you imagine if companies such as AT&T, Sprint, T-Mobile, or Verizon banned smart phone service to all conservatives because they disagreed with their political ideology or they were against a potential customer whose political stance on a particular controversial subject differed from their official viewpoint? It would be considered absurd.

Yet, that is precisely what is happening with our social media. They are attempting to limit our free speech, if conservative views are not a close match to their own socialist thinking.

Some of those, who work in high tech, are also adopting social media as a powerful tool for socialist and communist activism. They are taking up political stands against the U. S. Department of Defense (DOD), U. S. Customs and Border Protection (CBP), and Immigration and Customs Enforcement (ICE). These issue-oriented positions are sometimes part of a much larger ideological agenda and goals that include the desire to:

"... fundamentally remake both the power structure inside tech companies and the power dynamic between those firms and the communities in which they operate like San Francisco, Silicon Valley, and Seattle."[190]

You might ask: How do they hope to accomplish these fundamental objectives? It goes far beyond more extensive regulation of corporations by government. It involves these types of actions:

- Significantly boost taxes on corporations, while the companies continue to exist.
- Take control of the means of production.
- Eliminate and replace private corporations with public ownership of enterprises, or worker-owned cooperatives.
- Unionize high tech workers, who currently are employed as contractors.
- Organize workers as a class and recognize the socialist view of class warfare.
- Abolish the prevailing wage system.[191]

These political planks in the platform of some in high tech generally sound like 19th century Marxist rhetoric that we read earlier. Their ideas seem to surface as promoting both socialism and communism all over again in the 21st century.

As we consider the stated goals and objectives of these socialist thinkers in high tech, the words of writer and philosopher, George Santayana, quickly spring to mind:

"Those Who Do Not Learn History Are Doomed To Repeat It."[192]

Let's hope these high tech workers will learn from the abysmal history of socialism and communism and can avoid living through the misery, suffering, destruction, and death that socialist thinking has wreaked on the world over the last 300 hundred years or so.

One group formed in 2015 to engage high tech workers with San Francisco residents is the Tech Workers Coalition. According to the Fast Company website:

> "The Tech Workers Coalition has attracted a variety of activists, including communist revolutionaries. "More and more tech workers are unifying and organizing around a shared disillusionment with the entrepreneurial and libertarian ethos of Silicon Valley elites, and the realization that their interests are not the same as their bosses.""[193]

Indeed, many in high tech seem enamored with recycling the failed ideas of socialism and communism, both of which have proven to be dismal and depressing failures – spiritually, morally, political, economically, and personally for the average citizen.

The promotion of socialist thinking by some social media platforms and by some of those in high tech industry is one more reason that we see the current interest in socialism in America in the 21st century.

Let's look at Hollywood and the entertainment industry to understand another reason for the latest unwarranted attraction for socialism in America today.

Socialism Often Promoted by Hollywood and the Entertainment Industry

Without much question, Hollywood and the entertainment industry is a bulwark of across-the-board Leftist and socialist ideology. If you survey the landscape around Hollywood and the entertainment industry, you will typically find support for:

- Frequent and vociferous criticism of America,
- Stalwart and unshakeable support for many of America's enemies,
- A citadel and abutment for backing big government programs,
- A consistent proponent for failed Marxist economic principles, and
- A plethora of the usual socialist memes, such as climate change, radical and over-the-top environmentalism, and America as a hodgepodge group of victim classes.[194]

The history of socialist and communist thinking in Hollywood and the entertainment industry actually dates back to early in the 20th century. Back decades ago, Joseph Stalin was intrigued by the power of cinema to politically influence ordinary citizens for the socialist cause. Further, the Communist Party of the United States of America (CPUSA) was similarly taken by the use of movies and the entertainment industry to persuade people and to push propaganda aligned with communist ideas.[195]

Recall, too, the Soviet Union at the time was attempting to export socialism and communism around the world. In fact, the Soviet Union highly influenced the CPUSA, and in turn, the CPUSA influenced Hollywood.

One look at Hollywood and communism and socialism described events this way:

> "Communist cultural doctrine cast writers as "artists in uniform," producing works whose function was to transmit political messages and raise the consciousness of their audiences. Otherwise, movies were mere bourgeois decadence, a tool of capitalist distraction, and therefore subjugation." [196]

Involvement of the Communist Party in Hollywood included:

- Helping to organize the Screen Writer's Guild,
- Preventing some films from being produced when communists were hostile to the content,
- Initiating smear campaigns and blacklisting of non-communists – among those blacklisted were such well-known celebrities as Barbara Stanwyck, Bette Davis, and Lana Turner, and
- Characterizing life under communism without depicting the brutality that existed in the real world.[197]

One example of the influence of socialist and communist thinking on movies can be seen in the pro-Soviet propaganda film *Mission to Moscow.* In this movie, the ruthless dictator

Joseph Stalin was made to seem like a "benign and goodhearted leader." Russian citizens suffering from the ills of communism were portrayed as well off and happy in a grossly inaccurate depiction of their horrible conditions. Jonathan Leaf sums up the underlying message about life in the Soviet Union in the film:

> "Communism is a wholesome, benevolent system of government that only Nazi sympathizers would oppose."[198]

Incidentally, Ronald Reagan, at the time a liberal Democrat, was an anti-communist leader in Hollywood.[199]

To illustrate the Leftwing bias and socialist thinking in the larger entertainment industry, consider these examples:

- Leonard Goldberg, whose credits include executive producer of *Charlie's Angels* and *Starsky and Hutch,* when asked about whether or not there was a political barrier to entry in the TV industry, he was quoted as answering "Absolutely."
- Susan Harris, who was the creator of *Soap* and *Golden Girls,* described conservatives as "idiots" with "medieval minds."
- Discussing TV comedy, Fred Silverman, formerly in charge of ABC and subsequently NBC, clearly stated a bias with these words, "there's only one perspective, and it's a very progressive perspective."[200]

Given all these reasons, socialism has arisen from the ash heap of history once again, to mislead another generation, who has been deprived of learning history, politics, and economics. They have also not seen the benefits of freedom and free markets throughout their lives or possibly, they have taken those benefits for granted.

It is a grave mistake for the proponents of socialist thinking to assume that if capitalism is destroyed by the foolish and false promises of equality and fairness, then that prosperity will continue unabated.

Let's turn our attention next to the question of what potential strategy that socialists might use to make America a socialist country first, and then possibly a communist totalitarian dictatorship next.

Chapter 5

What is a Possible Strategy to Make America a Socialist Country and then Possibly a Communist Totalitarian Dictatorship

It is eminently clear that some socialists living in America today would much prefer living under socialism or communism to living in freedom. This fact is true despite a plethora of evidence that life is much better under capitalism, morality, individual freedom, and free markets, over and above anything that socialism, communism, and any totalitarian dictatorship can offer the average citizen. Of course, the elite under socialism live under a different set of laws and rules, and they are amply taken care of in a financial sense as well.

Because some socialists and communists appear to desire changing America from a Constitutional Republic endowed with a Bill of Rights and considerable freedoms to a new form of government – a socialist and possibly eventually a communist country, it's reasonable to expect that they might develop a detailed strategy and a specific set of plans to accomplish that objective.

The purpose of this chapter is to present a potential strategy that socialists and communists might use to convert America from a Constitutional Republic to a socialist form of government, followed by a communist country. This chapter is not meant to help socialists achieve their goals, but rather, it's hoped the Americans can learn what our nation potentially faces if socialists do attempt to change our wonderful political and economic system into the bottomless pit of socialism and communism.

All together the strategy this chapter presents consists of eight major points. Socialists might choose to use some, or all, or none, of these eight strategic points in developing a comprehensive overall strategy.

Let's study each of these eight points and learn how socialists might attempt to revolutionize our system of limited government, individual freedom and liberty into a socialist and then an ultimate communist totalitarian dictatorship.

Attack America's Judeo-Christian Heritage, Morality, and Freedom of Religion

America's greatest pillar of rock-solid strength is our Judeo-Christian heritage. Attacking America's Judeo-Christian heritage, our morality, and our Freedom of Religion would likely boost socialist efforts to move our nation toward socialism.

It's true,

- The Constitution – our outstanding political framework

- The Declaration of Independence – our remarkable moral framework, and
- Equality Under the Rule of Law – our vital legal framework

are all based upon our Judeo-Christian heritage. This, in turn, springs forth from our faith in God and our related faith in the Jewish faith and in the Christian faith.

This faith and the spiritual and moral wisdom taught in our synagogues and Churches and from the inspired Word of God in the Bible forms the foundation for our belief in the Truth that sets us free, and in our deeply held belief in the intrinsic human dignity and transcendent human value of every human person alive in America today and in every citizen alive in the entire world as well.

Our Judeo-Christian heritage also extends to our profound belief in the human dignity and deep-seated value of life in the womb. Hence, this faith in God manifests itself as a right to life from conception to natural death, and normally does not morally permit abortion, infanticide, or euthanasia.

Physician-assisted suicide (or medically-assisted suicide)[201] is another policy issue that socialists are more likely to support. People, who have faith in God, generally believe physician-assisted suicide is fundamentally immoral.

Socialist thinking, with its basis in atheism, usually rejects all or most of our Judeo-Christian heritage, as well as the morality associated with our faith in God that is based on the Bible, the Ten Commandments, Eternal Law, Divine Law, and Natural Law. To be valid, according to our theological understanding, Human Law needs to conform to the three higher laws - Eternal Law, Divine Law, and Natural Law.[202]

On the other hand, socialist thinking seems to not only accept, but sometimes even appears to actually relish, abortion, infanticide, or euthanasia, that are all thought to be immoral in our Judeo-Christian heritage.

Socialist thinking also typically rejects America's Freedom of Religion contained in the First Amendment to the Constitution. How? Socialists interfere with our Freedom of Religion by demanding a so-called, yet non-existent "wall of separation" between Church and State that does not exist in the original Constitution. It was read into the Constitution by a convoluted interpretation of the Establishment Clause by the Supreme Court in 1974.[203]

Socialists claim and expect that most (and probably nearly all) references to religion should be eliminated all over the nation because of this questionable interpretation dealing with the "wall of separation" between Church and State. To illustrate, consider a few examples:

- Prohibiting school children in public schools from wearing clothes with Bible verses,
- Prohibiting citizens from distributing Christian materials on a public sidewalk, and
- Banning references to God in public school graduation speeches.

These instances cited above deal with the free expression of a person's religion, a freedom that the Constitution specifically allows.

The First Amendment to the U. S. Constitution begins with these clear and concise words:

> "Congress shall make no law respecting an establishment of religion, or prohibiting the free exercise thereof; ..."

It is crucial to realize that this First Amendment applies to Congress and not to American citizens. It restricts Congress in matters relating to religion. For example, in the Establishment Clause, it prohibits Congress from selecting and establishing a religion for all of America to follow, a national religion. It also concisely restricts Congress in the Free Exercise Clause, from prohibiting any citizen from exercising and expressing his or her religion freely.

Nevertheless, socialists continue to attack our Freedom of Religion. They also continue to attack America's Judeo-Christian heritage and our traditional morality with their advocacy and support for relatively unrestricted abortion as well as in other matters that deal with moral questions. In some places, socialists even appear to support infanticide after a baby comes to term and there is a failed abortion attempt.

Attacking America's Judeo-Christian heritage, our morality, and our Freedom of Religion is just one point in a potential socialist strategy to move America from a Constitutional Republic living under freedom to a communist totalitarian dictatorship living under tyranny and oppression.

Next, let's look at the second point in this possible socialist strategy.

Attack America's Family Heritage – Traditional Family, Marriage, Life, and Sexual Identities

A second bedrock of America's strength and success as a nation is America's family heritage that includes: the traditional family unit (father, mother, and children); the traditional marriage between a man and woman; the transcendent and intrinsic value of each family member (including a baby growing in the womb of the mother); and the traditional sexuality and biological and sexual differences between a man and a woman.

Socialists challenge all these traditional family heritage concepts and attack the traditional family, the traditional marriage, the right to life of a baby in the mother's womb, and even the traditional sexuality of men and women. Socialists hope to attack and destroy America's family heritage, and in fact, are also attempting to attack and destroy the family heritage found in all of Western Civilization.

This particular second point of a potential socialist strategy to remake America into a socialist and then possibly a communist country is of value to socialists because it tears at the very fabric of traditional American life. Destroy the family and the stability of our current society is shaken, later shocked, and eventually over time goes into an emotional convulsion.

Some will argue that over the centuries, marriage has evolved and that is true. Initially, marriage was often for economic reasons or for procreating heirs. The Catholic Church in 1215 raised the status of marriage and its spiritual and moral significance to that of a sacrament, such as Baptism or Confirmation.[204]

But, in more recent years, marriage evolved into a means for finding love in permanent, monogamous, and sexual relationships. Traditional marriage is also civilization's arrangement and structure for raising children, and for protecting both children and wives.

It might surprise some that the animosity for the traditional family was also a central theme of Marxism. In Friedrich Engel's 1984 book, *The Origin of the Family, Private Property and the State,* he wrote about the family and in essence, class warfare, in these words:

> "The first class antagonism appearing in history coincides with the development of the antagonism of man and wife in monogamy, and the first class oppression with that of the female by the male sex."[205]

Indeed, the global sexual revolution with all its maladies that we are witnessing starts out with the socialist attack on the traditional family. In the socialist mindset, abolishing the family eliminates one source, the original source, of class warfare and moves a society closer to their desired classless utopia of so-called equality.[206]

This open hostility to the traditional family results in a number of modern pathologies we live with today, including the disintegration of the family in general; painfully broken families in particular; single parents struggling to raise their children completely alone and often in poverty; younger adults and even children, who suffer from dark spiritual anguish and profound emotional trauma; addicts hooked on pornography for the purpose of grasping at sexual pleasure; significant and untold numbers of sexual child abusers; and millions of tragically aborted babies. In fact, it is estimated that over 40 million babies around the world are aborted before they can be born every year.[207]

America's family heritage is based on monogamy. Under socialist thinking and advocacy, monogamy would give way to hedonism and sexual promiscuity in an attempt to create a communist society in the name of so-called equality, non-discrimination, and unrestricted sexual freedom.

It's true that many people can be seduced by the bogus appealing notion of unlimited sexual license, of free sex, without costs or responsibilities. But, the pathologies listed earlier are the real price of attacking and attempting to destroy America's traditional family heritage.

Next, let's think about the third point in a potential socialist strategy to move America from a Constitutional Republic living under freedom to a communist totalitarian dictatorship living under tyranny and oppression.

Attack America's Political Heritage – The Constitution and Freedom

Another source of America's superior strength and political resiliency is our incredible political heritage that is not duplicated anywhere else in the world. Our marvelous political heritage consists of two components that are inextricably linked together to provide an efficient and effective limited government and at the same time, unprecedented individual liberty and freedom, as well as economic opportunity, growth, and prosperity.

These two extraordinary and exceptional components of our political heritage are our Constitution and our Freedom that is protected by the Constitution.

It is no wonder that socialists, who seek to tear down our Constitutional Republic and replace it with socialism and ultimately communism, focus so much of their time, resources, and efforts on attacking the Constitution and our freedom.

The Constitution – A Vital Component of America's Political Heritage

Let's look first at our Constitution to appreciate how and why it creates such a practical and viable political framework. Federalism, the Presidential Electoral College, the separation of powers, and a system of checks and balances are all part of the remarkable political framework that guides and guards our nation and our freedom

Constitution – Created by the States and the Principle of Federalism

To begin with, remember that our Constitution was written by the States. They came together and formed the Federal government. Initially, the Federal government did not create the States.

Rather than permitting our Federal government unlimited power, the people of the United States often through the States retain the real power in America.

The Ninth and Ten Amendments in the Bill of Rights are clear on these limitations. The Ninth Amendment reads:

> "The enumeration in the Constitution of certain rights shall not be construed to deny or disparage others retained by the people."

The Ten Amendment is closely related and is expressed in these eloquent and profound words:

> "The powers not delegated to the United States by the Constitution, nor prohibited by it to the States, are reserved to the States respectively, or to the people."

By the way, recall that the Bill of Rights consists of the first ten Amendments to the Constitution and it was ratified on December 15, 1791.

This feature of the Constitution, also known as Federalism, served to disperse power among the States and at the same time to limit the scope and power of the Federal government to help assure that the Federal government didn't become too powerful or worse yet, a dictatorship.

Is it any wonder why socialists and communists don't like our Constitution, for that reason alone? It was designed not to be at the time, or ever to become in the future, a big powerful, centralized Federal government.

Constitution and the Presidential Electoral College

Supporting the principle of Federalism and assuring that all future Presidents and Vice Presidents do not necessarily come from just a handful of larger, more populated States, the Constitution assigns each State a number of presidential electors, which is equal to the total number of members of the U.S. House of Representatives from that State, added to the total number of members of the U. S. Senate from that same State.

The Twenty-Third Amendment to the Constitution, ratified on March 29, 1961, authorized the District of Columbia to also be allocated presidential electors, not to exceed the number of presidential electors given to the least populous State. The District of Columbia currently is given three presidential electors in the Presidential Electoral College every four years.

By the way, another element of Federalism embedded in the Constitution is the prohibition that both the President and Vice-President cannot be from the same State. This is another provision to help weaken any one State's power in the Federal government.

Constitution and the Separation of Powers

Another feature of the Constitution created to disperse power is the separation of powers among the three branches of the Federal government – namely, the Executive Branch, the Legislative Branch, and the Judicial Branch. Their roles are limited to these functions:

- Executive Branch (consists of the President, Vice-President, and various departments and agencies) – Enforce the Constitution and the laws of the land
- Legislative Branch (consists of the U. S. House of Representatives and the U. S. Senate) – Write the laws
- Judicial Branch (consists of the Supreme Court, Circuit Courts of Appeal, and the Federal District Courts) – Interpret the laws

Constitution and Checks and Balances

Along with the division of powers, the Constitution has a number of checks and balances built into our political structure. These checks and balance were designed to assure, once again, that no branch of the Federal government gets too powerful and rides roughshod over the other two branches. They were definitely arranged to circumscribe the powers of each branch of government.

How Might a Potential Socialist Strategy Attack America's Constitution?

One line of attack by socialists could be to attack the existence of the Presidential Electoral College, thereby increasing the power of the Federal government at the expense of decreasing the power of the sovereign States.

Without the Constitutional Presidential Electoral College, a few larger States by population size could dominate most of the smaller States. The reason for this is presidential elections would effectively be won, not by the States and their Electoral Votes, but rather by total popular vote nationally. The principle of Federalism would likely be the victim of such an attack.

Destroying the Electoral College also would likely result in enhancing the long-term socialist chances of getting and keeping the presidency in the hands of coastal elites living in the larger socialist enclaves of the East and West coasts and a few other progressive cities and counties in the United States.

Without the Electoral College, socialists could more easily maintain control of the Executive Branch, making presidential elections considerably less competitive.

Using another line of attack, socialists might choose to dramatically alter the separation of powers built into the Constitution and destroy the check and balances that are built into the system.   How might these tactics be accomplished?

For one thing, socialists might try to use the judiciary to legislate from the bench. For example, instead of merely interpreting the laws, judges who favored socialism might choose to develop new laws with their own particular rulings. This would be a violation of the true separation of powers.

It is also possible that socialists unhappy with Constitutional rulings by the Supreme Court might attempt to alter a future Supreme Court by adding more than nine justices to the high court. In this manner, they might hope to later "stack" the Supreme Court in their favor, if they subsequently took the White House.

When out of power, socialists might possibly attack a president, who supports the Constitution, to encroach upon the authority of the presidential office.

In another scheme, socialists might choose to reject the results of a presidential election and systematically sabotage a president with countless subpoenas and frivolous investigations. They might also use the judicial system to needlessly sue a president, attempting to resist nearly every action of an administration with harassing litigation. Finally, they might go so far as to impeach an existing president for ideological reasons, and not for any of the specific violations listed in Article II, Section 4 of the U. S. Constitution – namely, treason, bribery, or other high crimes and misdemeanors.

The second extraordinary and exceptional component of America's political heritage is our wonderful Freedom that is also protected by the Constitution.

Freedom – A Vital Component of America's Political Heritage

Attacking America's freedom is part of the third point in a potential socialist strategy to move America from a Constitutional Republic living under freedom to a communist totalitarian dictatorship living under tyranny and oppression.

To illustrate, consider our Freedom of Speech. In a free nation, Freedom of Speech is needed to learn and to understand, to question and to answer, to consider ideas and challenge policies, to make the best decisions for our lives, and for so much more as well.

As mentioned earlier in this chapter, Freedom of Religion is also critical to support our Judeo-Christian heritage, our morality, and our freedom to express our religious beliefs in public.

In recent years, some socialists have tried to circumvent our Freedom of Religion (and religious expression) with a limited (but positive-sounding) Freedom of Worship. This is a deceptive, hollow, and cosmetic ruse. Of course, Americans should be free to worship God as they choose (or not worship God if they choose). However, Freedom of Worship cannot substitute for Freedom of Religion and the freedom to express one's spiritual and moral beliefs freely in public. Our religious views need not be hidden in, or limited to, our places of worship, as Freedom of Worship might be seen to imply or interpreted by some socialists.

Another important area to protect Americans is in the realm of the Second Amendment. The Freedom to Keep and Bear Arms is manifestly necessary and clearly indispensable for two significant reasons. First, citizens must be able to protect themselves and their private property from harm or theft. Importantly, second, citizens must be able to protect themselves in case a future government was to become tyrannical. Arms are the last resort to protect Freedom from a totalitarian dictatorship.

Much research has been performed on guns and whether or not gun laws save more lives or cost more lives. One researcher, John Lott, known for his efforts to understand gun and crime statistics states that:

> "Allowing citizens to carry concealed handguns reduces violent crimes, and the reductions coincide very closely with the number of concealed handgun permits issued. Mass shootings in public places are

reduced when law-abiding citizens are allowed to carry concealed handguns."[208]

Also, it might be of potential interest that concealed handguns seem to protect women more so than men:

> "Guns also appear to be the great equalizer among the sexes. Murder rates decline when either more women or more men carry concealed handguns, but the effect is especially pronounced for women."[209]

According to the research, it turns out that a woman carrying a concealed handgun reduces the murder rate for women three to four times more than a man carrying a concealed handgun reduces the associated murder rate for men.[210]

Looking beyond the United States, it's also helpful to understand the correlation, if any, between banning guns and the murder rate. Once again, the need for the Second Amendment wins hands down. Consider a study reported on The Federalist's website.

While it's true that the number of guns owned in America per 100,000 citizens is the highest in the world, compared to low-ownership countries like El Salvador, Venezuela, and South Africa, it is also true that a gun in America is 387 times less likely to be used in a murder. The data go on to point out what might first appear to be a contradiction:

> "... it's worth considering why so many countries that have relatively successful programs of limiting private lawful ownership of guns are so dangerous and why

countries with such high rates of private gun ownership are relatively safe.[211]

The overall conclusion of this study is straight-forward: "... murders are less common when the victim might be armed."[212]

Let's consider how a potential socialist strategy might attack America's freedom. In particular, how might socialists possibly go on the offensive against our Freedom of Religion, Freedom of Speech, and our Freedom to Keep and Bear Arms?

How Might a Potential Socialist Strategy Attack America's Freedom?

We have already discussed a potential socialist attack strategy on our Freedom of Religion. Other potential attacks on our freedom include direct assaults on our Freedom of Speech, on our Freedom to Keep and Bear Arms, and other freedoms as well.

Freedom of Speech can be assailed in many ways. Some socialists might choose to shout down conservative speakers on college and university campuses. Some socialists might give lower grades to students, who voice their conservative views in classroom discussions or in thoughtful term papers or on tests.

Under some circumstances, socialists might decide to claim conservative idea are hate speech and cannot be spoken in public conversation. Politically correct, and politically limiting, speech might also become the target of socialists attacking our Freedom of Speech.

In addition to Freedom of Religion and Freedom of Speech, it goes without saying that some socialists seek to strip guns from the hands of gun owners throughout the United States. It is easy to imagine that socialists might choose to attack our Freedom to Keep and Bear Arms with any number of gun control measures, including:

- Onerous and more extensive background checks,
- "Red Flag" laws that take away weapons from citizens accused of being of potential harm to themselves or others, possibly with little or no due process before the gun confiscation,
- More extensive limitations on gun magazine sizes,
- More extensive limitations on types of weapons banned,
- More extensive limitations on semi-automatic weapons, and
- More gun-free zones that prohibit law-abiding citizens from carrying a gun inside the zone, but does virtually nothing to prevent a criminal for entering the zone with a weapon and ammunition

Taking away peaceful citizens Freedom to Keep and Bear Arms in a manner analogous to what took place by the National Socialists during the Nazi regime in Germany shows how socialists can wield authoritative control and consolidate repressive power using gun control laws.[213]

These are just a few examples of how a potential socialist attack strategy on our Constitution and freedom might take place. Of course, other strategies and plans might be developed over time.

Let's think about the next point, the fourth point, in a potential socialist strategy to move America from a Constitutional Republic living under freedom to a socialist country and then possibly a communist totalitarian dictatorship living under tyranny and oppression.

Attack America's Rule of Law – Create One Set of Laws for the Socialist Elite and One Set of Laws for Regular Citizens

One of the truly great aspects of life in America has been the confidence of ordinary citizens to be treated fairly in the American judicial system. "Equality under the Rule of Law" has been the principle under which citizens have lived for over two centuries.

With the Rule of Law, laws need to be promulgated publically. Secret laws, in contrast, cannot fairly be expected to be followed by the people when they are not known. Laws also need to be applied equally to all citizens, not just a select few. Finally, laws should be interpreted by a judiciary whose personal views are independent of the citizen or citizens involved in the case.

In their efforts to obtain, keep, and solidify power, socialists might attack the Rule of Law that stands as the foundation of American jurisprudence. They might choose, if they are able, to create a two-tiered system of justice – with one set of laws for the socialist elite and one set of laws for regular citizens.

Alternatively, socialists might try, if possible, to keep one set of laws for everyone, but only enforce or prosecute the laws for regular citizens. In this way, socialist elite could get away with breaking the laws with impunity because they would not be brought to justice.

Not surprisingly, these types of socialist tactics would likely require help from either socialist prosecutors or socialist judges or both. Completely impartial prosecutors and judges would tend to stick with the Rule of Law and the socialists involved would be frustrated being treated as regular citizens.

The fifth point for a potential strategy for socialists seeking to move America from a Constitutional Republic living under freedom, to a socialist country, and then possibly a communist totalitarian dictatorship living under tyranny and oppression, deals with American elections.

Attack America's Election System – Eliminate the Presidential Electoral College, Make It Easier to Conduct Voter Fraud, Allow Non-Citizens to Vote, Use Vote Harvesting, and Use Ranked-Choice Voting

A fifth point in a potential socialist strategy to move America to socialism and communism is to tamper with America's Election System.

According to the United States Geological Survey, there are 3,141 counties or county equivalents in the United States. That includes:

- 3,007 Actual Named Counties (across the country)
- 16 Boroughs (in Alaska)
- 11 Census Areas that are not Boroughs (in Alaska)
- 64 Parishes (in Louisiana)
- 42 Independent Cities (1 in Maryland, 1 in Missouri, 1 in Nevada, and the remainder in Virginia)[214]

The significance of this large number of counties is that most counties hold their own separate elections and are part of the large, rather extensive, and geographically dispersed network that is America's Election System.

Incidentally, every four years, lots of media coverage and pundit discussion are focused on the presidential election. It's often treated as one single election. Most national polls report on the likelihood of the candidates' chances of winning that singular election. However, our presidential election is not one simple election won by the popular vote nationally.

Technically, among the 50 states, 48 states are normally winner-take-all Electoral Votes elections, based on the popular vote in each of the respective and independent State elections. Maine and Nebraska allocate Electoral Votes in a different manner. These States award Electoral Votes by a combination of winner-take-all and by Congressional districts. In these two states only, two Electoral Votes are allocated to the winner of the State popular vote and one Electoral Vote is allocated to the popular vote winner in each Congressional district.[215]

The Electoral College vote ultimately determines the winner of a presidential election. It's really 56 elections and technically should be studied with 50 State polls plus polls for the District of Columbia and the five individual Congressional districts that comprise Maine and Nebraska, not one national poll.[216]

One strength of our presidential elections is the fact that it's conducted using the Presidential Electoral College. It gives each State and the District of Columbia the opportunity to participate individually and to select a president based on local and regional needs.

Another strength of our elections is the distributed nature of individual county elections. It's more difficult to commit fraud in over 3,000 distinct geographically dispersed elections than in one centralized Federal government system (that we fortunately don't have).

So, how might socialists attack America's Election System? One way was mentioned earlier. That tactic was to attack the Presidential Electoral College and to try to eliminate it from the Constitution.

A closely related potential tactic for socialists to employ would be to push a National Popular Vote Interstate Compact (NPVIC) that would have each participating State give their Electoral Votes to the popular vote winner nationally, rather than to the candidate that carried their particular State.[217]

This National Popular Vote approach might not pass Constitutional muster in the Supreme Court, however. Obviously, it's a violation of the system originally built into the Constitution. Also, it can be asserted that such a compact is not constitutional because an Amendment to the

Constitution was not first approved under Article V of the Constitution. Article 5 presents the details of the Constitutional Amendment process.

If enough States pass such a law despite the Constitutional questions surrounding such an interstate compact, the presidential election in question will certainly be tied up in the courts for quite some time. It might generate a Constitutional debate at the least, and it might trigger a deep Constitutional crisis at worst.

Parenthetically, the trigger point for the National Popular Vote Interstate Compact would be when enough States with Electoral Votes equaling or exceeding 270 approve the compact and their Electoral Votes could carry a presidential election in theory.

As of Fall 2019, 15 States plus the District of Columbia have passed the NPVIC. These 16 jurisdictions account for a total of 196 Electoral Votes.[218]

Another potential tactic for socialists is to attack America's Election System by making voter fraud easier to commit and allowing non-citizens to vote. Socialists might reason it would make it simpler for illegal immigrants, non-citizens, and other ineligible people to vote. Socialists might believe that the demographics of these groups would lend themselves more to socialist rhetoric. Therefore, in their view, these groups would be more likely to support and to vote for grandiose promises of generous government and other welfare benefits in the future.

While many socialists and progressives claim voter fraud is non-existent, rare, or minimal, the facts stand in sharp contrast. Examples of actual voter fraud abound and certainly, socialists fixated on changing America can attack America's Election System by making voter fraud much easier to commit and by encouraging or permitting non-citizens to vote.

Consider, first, the many different ways voter fraud can be committed by people set on changing the outcomes of America's elections:

- Impersonation of legitimate voters at the polls, or impersonating voters, who have died, moved, of become felons (the latter in locations that restrict felons from voting),
- False registrations of voters with a phony name, address, or location,
- Duplicate voting in the same location, or voting in multiple locations, during the same election,
- Fraudulent use of absentee ballots in a variety of different ways,
- Buying votes,
- Illegal assistance by forcing or intimidating or misleading voters, especially the elderly, disabled, illiterate, or those whose second language is English,
- Illegible voting by non-citizens or those not eligible to vote, such as felons, and
- Altering the vote count at a precinct or at a centralized location.[219]

In addition, here are just a handful of voter fraud cases:

- In California, the State disclosed that it had registered 25,000 ineligible voters,
- In Pennsylvania, the Department of Motor Vehicles registered thousands of non-citizens to vote, and
- In Michigan, the Detroit metro area registered 1,414 non-citizens in part because the State does not have a false citizenship claim (during voter registration) system.[220]

But, the numbers might be even more alarming that these few small examples indicate. One study in 2012 by the Pew Center on the States found incredibly that 1.8 million dead people were registered to vote, along with 2.75 million people, who were registered to vote in more than one State. Overall, the Pew study made a shocking conclusion:

> "The Pew report found that 24 million registrations were either invalid or inaccurate, making the registration systems vulnerable to fraud."[221]

An important point to make in this discussion (that might be overlooked by some) is when non-citizens vote, they are diluting the votes of American citizens. Two issues arise directly from this fact. First, if a State legislature apportions election districts on total population (citizens and non-citizens), citizens are at risk of losing their fair representation in their own districts. Second, at the Federal government level, some believe that resources are being directed to States with greater non-citizen populations.

Two additional tactics that socialist might choose to utilize to attack America's Election System are promoting "vote harvesting" and "ranked-choice voting." These are both tools that can significantly alter the results of elections.

Vote harvesting might seem innocuous at first. But, it can be deployed with destructive results. Vote harvesting is a provision in some election laws for giving third parties the right to pick up absentee ballots from individual voters, collect them together, and then return them to election officials.[222] To illustrate, a partisan campaign worker might visit 100 senior citizens, pick up their absentee ballots, and subsequently, drop them off at a county courthouse.

While the idea of vote harvesting might seem reasonable on its face, it is nevertheless ripe for voter fraud. One election researcher and expert puts it this way:

> "Neither voters nor election officials can verify that the secrecy of the ballot was not compromised or that the ballot submitted in the voter's name by a third party accurately reflects the voter's choices and was not fraudulently changed by the vote harvester. And there is no guarantee that vote harvesters won't simply discard the ballots of voters whose political preferences for candidates of the opposition party are known."[223]

Also, there is no way to assure a voter has not been influenced, coerced, threatened, or intimidated during the vote harvesting process.[224]

Another tactic for attacking America's Election System is to promote ranked-choice voting (also, known as "instant runoff" voting). With this election ruse, instead of voting for your first choice for office, you rank all the candidates from your first choice to your last choice.

If the candidate with the most first choice votes doesn't achieve a majority, then that candidate is eliminated from running, and all the candidate's first choice voters, those who voted for the now eliminated first choice candidate, have their first choice votes changed to their second choices. This elimination and re-voting procedure continues until one candidate gets a majority of the votes.

This election ploy is awkward, cumbersome, and can result in marginal candidates getting elected. It also works against choosing the best candidate and making an informed decision because it is a complex and convoluted approach. Plus, in practice, some voters don't bother voting more than a first or second choice. It's too much bother for them.

To sum up this fifth point in a potential socialist strategy to convert America into a socialist and then communist country is to attack America's Elections System by some combination of tactics that include:

- Eliminate the Presidential Electoral College,
- Make it easier to conduct voter fraud,
- Allow non-citizens to vote,
- Promote vote harvesting, and
- Promote ranked-choice voting.

The sixth point for a potential strategy for socialists seeking to move America from a Constitutional Republic living under freedom to a communist totalitarian dictatorship living under tyranny and oppression deals with America's Sovereign Borders.

Attack America's Sovereign Borders – Allow Unlimited Illegal Immigration, Promote Sanctuary Cities and States, Expand the Number of Socialist Voters, and Change America's Culture

Another portion of a possible socialist strategy to harm America, bring down our 242+ year Constitutional Republic, and attempt to install a socialist country, followed quickly by a communist dictatorship, is to attack America's Sovereign Borders and permit unlimited illegal immigration.

This open border strategy places an undue burden on America's financial resources – welfare costs, education costs, and costs related to both actual crimes and criminal enforcement.

Take, for example, a report from the Texas Department of Public Safety that details from June 1, 2011 through July 31, 2019 that about 297,000 non-citizens were booked into local Texas jails, 202,000 of those were later determined to be illegal immigrants. In total, this group was charged with approximately 494,000 criminal offenses over the course of their criminal careers.[225]

While some of these criminal offenses might still be actively prosecuted, there have been about 225,000 convictions so far including these specific crimes:

- 500 homicides,
- 23,954 assaults,
- 8,070 burglaries,
- 297 kidnappings,
- 14,178 thefts,
- 2,026 robberies,
- 3,122 sexual assaults,
- 3,840 sexual offenses,
- 3,158 weapon charges, and
- Tens of thousands of drug and obstruction charges.[226]

All of these crimes can have both considerable human costs as well additional costs incurred by the justice system. In addition to these crime related expenses, what about all the other expenses that illegal immigration causes?

According to a study by the Federation for American Immigration Reform (FAIR), the Federal, State, and local costs for illegal immigration equals an enormous $116 Billion annually.[227]

In September 2019, President Trump tweeted his own even greater assessment of illegal immigration costs: "Illegal Immigration costs the USA over 300 Billion Dollars a year."[228]

Although the sheer costs associated with an open border strategy and illegal immigration are prohibitively high, socialists might attack America's Sovereign Borders primarily for other reasons.

One benefit socialists and communists might like to see is the ability to expand the voter rolls with relatively poor, uneducated, and unemployed illegal immigrants – many with medical issues and most unable to speak English, even as a second language. In the view of some observers, these illegal immigrants would probably cast votes over 90% of the time for socialist promises of free benefits, if permitted to vote.

Of course, many socialists probably might push to allow these needy non-citizens to legally vote, or alternatively, to gain citizenship quickly for the same reason. In fact, some socialists already think strongly that illegal immigrants should vote when they are already living in a given community.

Of course, as data presented earlier illustrate, some non-citizens flagrantly violate election registration laws and vote prior to becoming citizens anyway. When caught voting this way, some non-citizens then even claim that they were unaware that they are not allowed to vote until they become naturalized citizens.[229]

Another related tactic socialists might choose to follow is to support and to encourage sanctuary cities and States. Why? Because sanctuary cities and States resist the Federal government's efforts to deport known criminals and therefore, voter rolls might once again swell further.

Obviously, if they choose to promote sanctuary cities and States, socialists don't care if criminals stay in the United States as a result of foolish sanctuary policies. Such sanctuary policies place American citizens at risk of being victims of crimes perpetrated by illegal immigrants convicted of previous crimes within the United States.

Ultimately, this potential tactic, attacking America's Sovereign Borders, would accomplish something profound. It would help to change America's "Culture of Freedom" to a completely different mindset, a "Culture of Entitlement." This change would move America from a culture that used individual freedom and liberty to innovate and to build and to prosper, to a giant welfare state and a culture that expects everything handed to citizens and non-citizens by the big, centrally planned Federal government.

In the process, Americans would lose a considerable amount of freedom and those seeking their entitlements would learn that those socialist grandiose promises were never delivered anyway. Those promises were actually well-concocted, dishonest fabrications, and phony lies.

The next, seventh point, in a potential strategy for socialists seeking to move America from a Constitutional Republic living under freedom to a communist totalitarian dictatorship living under tyranny and oppression deals with America's economic freedom and prosperity.

Attack America's Economic Freedom and Prosperity – With High Taxes, Fiscal Irresponsibility, Burdensome Regulations, and Inflation to Redistribute Wealth

The recipe for economic growth, opportunity, and prosperity is well known. It starts with economic freedom in a climate that is conducive to economic growth. It includes these types of factors:

- Low taxes on economic growth including capital formation and income,
- Regulatory restraint (minimal regulations, except for safety),
- Fiscal restraint (balanced budgets and better management of national debt),
- Monetary restraint (strong dollar, rule-based monetary policy, low inflation policy),
- Private property,
- Rule of Law (including enforcement of contracts),
- Free enterprise (including ease of starting a new business)
- Free markets (including no wage and price controls, no government selection of winners and losers),
- Free and fair trade with other nations,
- Stability of Federal and state government policies, and
- Peace at home and abroad.

For readers that want to delve into economic freedom and prosperity in more detail than is possible in this book, including:

- How to create economic growth?
- How to create prosperity?

Please consider reading my 2014 book: *Renewing America and Its Heritage of Freedom: What Freedom-Loving Americans Can Do To Help.*[230]

Socialists, who wish to damage America, on a road to socialism and totalitarianism, might decide to attack America's economic freedom and prosperity. Alternatively, they might choose to follow such an attack strategy in their false hopes of obtaining the so-called benefits of socialism directly.

For example, socialists might think that high marginal tax rates on capital formation and high taxes on income will move the American Economy toward a more egalitarian society. They also might think that easy money and high inflation created through poor monetary policies will assist the socialist elite in redistributing the nation's wealth.

Sadly for those who succumb to socialist economic rhetoric, the realities of socialism and communism and the abject poverty they create, catches up with their failed economic theory and practice.

Recall from Chapter 1 that socialism always leads on a path to spiritual, moral, and economic bankruptcy. Sometimes, of course, actual bankruptcy is avoided by adopting free market and capitalist principles before it is too late. Then, it can no longer be called socialism; it's capitalism that's running the nation in question.

The eighth and final point in a potential strategy for socialists seeking to move America from a Constitutional Republic living under freedom to a communist totalitarian dictatorship living under tyranny and oppression deals with making grandiose promises to give away free things in order to get votes.

Make Grandiose Promises to Give Away Free Things to Get Votes – Win Elections, But Fail to Deliver on the Big Lies and Phony Promises

The final possible strategy that socialists might choose to follow to move America toward socialism and communism can be called the "Santa Clause Strategy." Simply, in order to win elections, socialists need to garner votes. In the minds of some socialists, making grandiose promises is an election-winning strategy.

What might be included in the list of freebies promised by socialists, who decide on using the Santa Clause Strategy? Here are some planks a potential socialist election platform might contain:

- Free Medical Care,
- Free Dental Care,
- Free Vision Care,
- Free Home Care Services,
- Free Long-Term Care Services,
- Free Psychological Counseling Services,
- Free Forgiveness of All Medical Debt,
- Free Child Care,
- Free School Breakfasts and Lunches,
- Free College Tuition,
- Free Trade School Tuition,
- Free Forgiveness of All Student Debt,
- Free (or Affordable) Housing,
- Free Jobs with Living Wages,
- Free Basic Income,

- Free Basic Phone Service,
- Free Basic Cable TV Service,
- Free Basic Internet Service, and
- Free Basic Transportation Service.

Note that all these freebies come with a significant price tag that will be difficult or impossible to pay for completely. If elected to office, socialists would probably need to consider:

- Charging outrageously high tax rates on the rich and middle class,
- Increasing the national debt to enormously steep levels,
- Increasing inflation (a potential tax on the poor, who can least afford inflation) through monetary policy to pay for some of the freebies with a devalued currency, and
- Altering fiscal and regulatory policies to force-fit bad economic decisions on a burdened American Economy.

While the Santa Clause Strategy will sound good to some citizens that are seduced by the unrealistic promises, many other citizens will be skeptical of the grandiose socialist rhetoric, and will be reluctant to pay for socialism with its extraordinarily high taxes and with the loss of much of their freedom.

The Bottom Line
As we pointed out earlier, it is eminently clear that some socialists living in America today would much prefer living

under socialism or communism to living in a Constitutional Republic in freedom.

Because some socialists and communists appear to desire changing America from a Constitutional Republic endowed with a Bill of Rights and considerable freedoms to a new form of government – a socialist and eventually a communist country, it's reasonable to expect that they might develop a detailed strategy and a specific set of plans to accomplish that objective.

A potential strategy that socialists and communists might use to convert America from a Constitutional Republic to a socialist form of government, followed by a communist country might include some combination of these eight major strategic points:

- Attack America's Judeo-Christian Heritage, Morality, and Freedom of Religion,
- Attack America's Family Heritage – Traditional Family, Marriage, Life, and Sexual Identities,
- Attack America's Political Heritage – The Constitution and Freedom,
- Attack America's Rule of Law,
- Attack America's Election System,
- Attack America's Sovereign Borders,
- Attack America's Economic Freedom and Prosperity, and
- Make Grandiose Promises to Give Away Free Things to Get Votes – The Santa Clause Strategy.

All together this chapter presents eight major strategic points that might make up some, or all, or none of a potential socialist strategy that they might utilize to try to revolutionize our system of limited government, individual freedom and liberty into an ultimate communist totalitarian dictatorship.

Chapter 6

Why Do Some People Find Socialism So Appealing and Seductive When the Evidence Indicates Capitalism is a Much Better System?

Despite the sordid history and abysmal track record of socialism over its roughly three centuries of existence, there are still many proponents of socialism hoping to inflict the spiritual, moral, and economic bankruptcy of socialism on their country or the entire world, without ever realizing the likely results of imposing such socialism on their respective targets.

Obviously, socialism finds a welcome home in the ivory towers of many American universities and colleges as well as in the halls of countless K-12 public schools in the U. S. It is also promoted in a diverse array of venues, spanning the mainstream media, social media, Hollywood, and both the high tech and entertainment industries. That considerable variety and level of biased opinion is bound to impact the recipients of this socialist rhetoric and also expand the message's extensive reach across America's substantial number of communication channels.

This chapter looks at the specious messages being sent by socialists across these various communications channels and why this spurious socialist rhetoric is both appealing and seductive to some citizens.

Let's look at one argument socialists use to criticize capitalism, namely income inequality and wealth inequality among its citizens. Socialists want to eliminate both income inequality and wealth inequality in the name of so-called fairness.

Some People Incorrectly Believe Socialism Will Help to Eliminate Income Inequality and Wealth Inequality among Citizens

In free markets under capitalism, socialists condemn the twin notions of income inequality and wealth inequality. Socialists believe that it's fundamentally unfair for some people to be paid significantly more than other people, or to have substantially more wealth than others. For example, why should a CEO earn $1 Million a year, while a factory worker in the same company only gets paid $50,000 a year? The $1 Million compensation is 20 times greater than the factory worker's pay.

This type of socialist rhetoric appeals to some workers, who think they don't make enough money. This is not surprising. Socialism often divides up citizens into various groups and then pits one group against another group. In the process, socialist rhetoric generates friction, animosity, antagonism, and sometimes even hatred.

Of course, if we look back at Marxism and its emphasis on class struggle, this class envy and class antagonism reaction makes complete sense.

One important question to ask is whether or not income inequality is bad or not. We can observe examples in the real world for insight.

In nature, differences and variations enrich life, empower life, and propel life forward. In contrast, uniformity is a close cousin of mediocrity.[231]

To illustrate further, consider the atmosphere that surrounds our planet. As the earth rotates through its annual orbital trajectory, the sun unevenly heats the earth's atmosphere and surfaces. The earth's tilt and the very shape of the earth itself also contribute to this uneven heating. The temperature differences, or thermal variations as some might prefer to call them, generate powerful barometric pressure gradients. Note that the term gradient is just another word for difference.

In turn, these pressure differences manifest themselves as Highs and Lows in the earth's atmosphere and big letter H's and L's on the weather maps we see on TV and computer screens. These H's and L's drive our short term weather, our long term climate, and also maintain a healthy energy balance across the earth.

The bottom line in this example is that these temperature and pressure differences are built into the fabric of our life and human existence on the earth.

Let's consider another example. Integrated circuits and the electronic products we live with every day rely on a natural phenomenon known as electricity.

In fact, electricity is another reality, driven on differences that exist in our natural world. Physicists and electronic engineers (EE's) call these potential differences. Such differences in electric potential between two locations in a circuit drive electric current. Without these potential differences, our smart phones, tablets, and notebook computers, would not function.

Finally, think about one last example, the differences between men and women. They are truly different. Both sexes are naturally unique, special, and different in their own God created ways. In fact, these biological and sexual differences enliven and enrich our lives. They make life more challenging, more rewarding, and certainly, more enjoyable.

Without the differences built into life by God, life would be rather dull, routine, and listless without the bright, colorful differences we see all around us in our lives and in nature.

Now, let's return to the debate over income and wealth inequality. The economics of life works in much the same way as the differences we find in the natural world.

Income inequality is a favorite socialist pejorative term, that means, income difference. Socialists believe that all citizens (except possibly governing socialist elites) should receive the same income, regardless of education, knowledge, expertise, special skills, experience, performance, productivity, or shortage of talent in a particular field. This is an utterly foolish idea.

Why should a brain surgeon be paid the same as a restaurant cook? Why should a CEO responsible for a $10 Billion budget, an employee workforce of 40,000 workers, and a global corporate strategy, who works 80 hours per week, be paid the same as a computer software engineer that works as an individual contributor on one project about 40 hours a week?

This is not meant to criticize a restaurant cook or a computer software engineer. Both are important jobs. But, most people would likely think the brain surgeon and the CEO are entitled to receive higher compensation in their respective professional roles.

Income inequality or more precisely income differences among competing businesses or between different individuals inspire entrepreneurs to create faster, better, and cheaper products and services.

Income differences also motivate individuals to improve their education, knowledge, expertise, special skills, experience, performance, and productivity to do a superior job, or to interview for a new job, and subsequently, to boost their own income for themselves and their families.

Income differences can create healthy motivation for, and solid competition among, individuals, entrepreneurs, and businesses alike.

Noted economist, Ludwig von Mises, reflecting on the importance of income and wealth inequality for economic growth states that:

> "Even those who look upon the inequality of wealth and incomes as a deplorable thing, cannot deny that it makes for progressing capital accumulation. And it is additional capital accumulation alone that brings about technological improvement, rising wage rates, and a higher standard of living."[232]

Indeed, it is income and wealth differences that drive economic growth and new wealth creation in our economy. It is socialists that deplore these differences, not capitalists.

There is another dimension to the income inequality debate. Income inequality is not a permanent condition by any means. Socialist rhetoric implies an income gap, once created, is constant from that time forward. That's simply not consistent with the data.

The American Economy is vibrant and is definitely not static. The dynamic nature of capitalism means that someone with a low or middle income one day can become a financial success essentially overnight. There are countless stories of individuals with brilliant new ideas, who became millionaires when their ideas were commercialized and brought to market.

In a similar way, many creative entertainers have become instant pop stars, amassing fortunes in just a period of a few months or years. With capitalism, upward economic mobility is not only possible, but it happens all the time.

The reverse is true too. Companies that were once great successes can get out of touch with their customers. They can move from profitability to lackluster performance in a short period of time. They sometimes are even forced to file for bankruptcy, when their products and services don't meet the needs of customers. Capitalism punishes businesses, products, and services that don't meet customer's needs or that waste scarce and expensive economic resources. When resources are wasted, prices go up and sales drop. Consumers find more cost effective products elsewhere.

Consider, too, some facts about upward economic mobility with capitalism in America. According to social scientist Arthur C. Brooks:

> "The U.S. Census Bureau, the Urban Institute, and the Federal Reserve have all pointed out that, as a general rule, about a fifth of the people in the lowest income quintile will climb to a higher quintile within a year, and that about half will rise within a decade. ... Millions and millions of poor Americans climb out of the ranks of poverty every year."[233]

In other words, if we break all incomes into quintiles (that is, five buckets with the same number of people in each bucket), 20% of individuals will move out of the bottom income quintile within one year and 50% of individuals will move out within 10 years. That's considerable upward income mobility. In America, individuals move out of poverty rather dramatically.[234]

Capitalism will rescue more people from poverty, absent burdensome government interference, than socialism can ever hope to rescue with their destructive economic policies.

In his research, Arthur C. Brooks found that instead of income equality causing happiness, happiness is really caused when individuals think that they have a chance of moving upward economically. Opportunity and upward economic mobility are the keys to happiness, as opposed to socialism's false promise of income equality.[235]

So, both upward and downward economic mobility are possible with capitalism. Income differences and wealth differences drive the dynamic creation and destruction of products, services, jobs, professions, businesses, and sometimes entire industries. Political economist Joseph A. Schumpeter captured this dynamic nature of capitalism with the phrase "Creative Destruction." In his words:

> "Capitalism, then, is by nature a form or method of economic change and not only never is but never can be stationary. ... This process of Creative Destruction is the essential fact about capitalism."[236]

In contrast, socialists seek uniformity, not diversity. When you think of it, that's rather odd given the lip-service some socialists give to diversity. Their idea of diversity involves diversity only when it promotes class struggles and other politically-correct, socialist thinking.

In particular, socialists seek the elimination of inequality in income and the elimination of inequality in wealth among all people. But, without these differences, there is no motivation to create economic growth and wealth.

Without inequality in income and wealth, the Free Market would collapse because these differences drive motivation, competition, and growth. If everyone received the same income and had the same level of wealth, what incentive would people have to do better, or for that matter, what incentive would people have to do anything at all? Plus, what incentives would entrepreneurs and businesses have to create new, faster, better, and cheaper products and services?

Additionally, if no one worked at all and if nothing new were ever created, the entire economy would collapse.

Incidentally, because socialism tends to destroy many economic incentives, that's the reason why socialism needs control, coercion, compulsion, and sometimes even violence to force people to do what they want them to do.

Capitalism, in sharp contrast, relies on economic incentives to achieve free, mutual, and peaceful cooperation. Without economic incentives, socialism relies on government-dictated control, coercion, compulsion, and in some cases violence to force human action.

Some socialists want to eliminate wealth inequality (or wealth differences) among citizens by nationalizing industries and creating worker-owned cooperatives. They say that this would take away the concentration of wealth from the hands of a few capitalists and put more control into the hands of workers.

Of course, this idea ignores the fact that many corporations are owned by stockholders and mutual fund owners. Lots of grandmothers are smart investors in the stock market and mutual funds.

This socialist scheme fails for a number of reasons. First, wealth is created in the private sector, never in the public sector. But, wealth is only consumed in the public sector, after it is first taxed away from the private sector.

Second, capitalists consist of many different kinds of small, medium, and large investors as well as venture capitalists, who specialize in start-up and small companies just beginning to grow. These private sector investors are much more adept at making prudent and careful investments with their own money or their client's capital, than are public sector bureaucrats.

Creating worker-owned cooperatives or running nationalized industries will likely result in much less efficient and cost effective use of scarce economic resources. A nation will be poorer as a result.

Indeed, if welfare state socialists achieve their twin goals of the elimination of income inequality and the elimination of wealth inequality, the result will be the elimination of economic growth and the elimination of wealth creation. This will quickly lead to capital consumption, to a declining standard of living, to economic poverty, and eventually to utter destitution, if not stopped and reversed in time.

Socialism can't eliminate inequality in income and wealth without consuming more wealth and creating more poverty.

Let's next look at another argument socialists use to criticize capitalism, economic injustice and the exploitation of workers. Socialists claim that they can help to eliminate economic injustice and the so-called exploitation of workers.

Some People Incorrectly Believe Socialism Will Help to Eliminate Economic Injustice and the Exploitation of Workers

Before we can address the question of whether or not socialism can help to eliminate economic injustice and the exploitation of workers, we need to challenge the underlying assumptions implicit in socialism's criticism of capitalism above.

First, are workers generally exploited under capitalism? Second, if workers are usually exploited under capitalism, do they experience economic injustice? Third, if workers are usually exploited under capitalism and they do experience economic injustice, can socialism help to eliminate that economic injustice?

Inherent in socialist theory is a critical concept that forms the basis of the theory of worker exploitation. It is fundamentally flawed, and economically unsound, and socially wrong. What is it?

Socialists assume incorrectly that owners of the means of production in the private sector are exploiting workers because the product or service produced creates a profit. The owners, of course, can be entrepreneurs, business owners, investors, stockholders, mutual fund investors, venture capitalists, angel investors, etc. Socialists call these private sector owners capitalists.

The total investment from all sources of investor funds goes to obtain the necessary means of production, including such items as land, office buildings, furniture, plant and machinery, and other capital equipment. Some investment dollars also are required for working capital to buy raw materials and other supplies.

Labor costs are vital as well; people require salaries or wages to do the work and create the product or service, often weeks or months before revenues begin to flow into the business.

Often overlooked in the capital expenditures necessary to launch or maintain a business is the Intellectual Property (IP) associated with the product or service. IP can be copyrights, patents, trade secrets, trademarks, licenses, etc. In a sense, a corporate business strategy or an innovative business model can both be additional forms of Intellectual Property.

Two other costs to figure into the investment equation are sweat equity and the cost of risk. All the investors are risking their capital in the business. Capital always has opportunity costs. An investor can place their money in a modest interest-bearing account or into a stock or equity position with low risk and a high dividend yield.

Recapping quickly those costs to bring a product or service to market:

- Sweat Equity of the Owners, Entrepreneurs, Angel Investors, and Venture Capitalists

- Risk of Capital Invested from All Investors
- Intellectual Property
  - Copyrights
  - Patents
  - Trade Secrets
  - Trademarks
  - Licenses
  - Business Strategy
  - Business Models
- Working Capital
  - Labor
  - Raw Materials
  - Supplies
- Land
- Office Buildings
- Furniture
- Plant
- Machinery
- Other Capital Expenditures (CAPEX)

Socialists incorrectly assume that the profit a product or service generated above the investment costs all are the result of labor alone, without regard to the many other factors listed above that are vital to making a profit, if any profit is actually made. After all, some businesses, products, and services don't make a profit and do lose money.

Using Marxist terminology, socialists call this value created over and above the investments made, the surplus value of labor. Socialist rhetoric then claims that it's economic injustice for owners to keep the so-called "surplus value of labor."

Socialists also err by oversimplifying capitalism into two major groups or categories of people in a capitalism economy – owners and workers.[237] In general, owners and workers are not monolithic economic groups that are actively involved in a class struggle or economic competition.

Rather, owners are individuals with unique needs and wants. Owners are in competition with other owners in the marketplace to win over customers and attempt to pay their bills and the salaries and wages of their workers. They hope to make a profit too. If they don't make a profit, they will sooner or later be forced to shut down and will have to let their workers go. Owners are not in direct competition with workers.

Just like owners, workers are unique individuals with their own special needs and wants. Individual workers bring their own specific education, knowledge, expertise, special skills, experience, performance, and productivity to the marketplace. Workers compete with other workers for the best jobs, salaries and wages, and benefits. Workers are not in direct competition with owners.

Socialists miss another related salient point. The private ownership of the means of production is in the best interest of both the owners and the workers.[238]

Ironically, over the centuries, socialists have had to work hard to try to convince workers that socialism and the public ownership of property might be of interest to them.[239] The idea of socialism has been thrust on mostly disinterested workers by socialists pushing their rhetoric on those individuals, who generally didn't appear to have much eagerness to try out socialism, let alone enough passion to seek out revolutionary or evolutionary change.

Returning to our earlier questions in this section, workers are not generally exploited under capitalism. In fact, their standard of living is likely higher than over the usual public ownership of the means of production options, namely, nationalization of industries and corporations converted to worker-owned cooperatives.

Since workers are not exploited, the answer to the second question is that they do not generally experience economic injustice under capitalism.

Finally, socialism can't help to improve the economic life of workers, since socialism would likely damage workers' economic interests under the public ownership of the means of production. They certainly can't eliminate economic injustice that doesn't exist.

Let's turn our attention to a third argument socialists use to criticize capitalism, corporate greed. Socialists claim that they can help to eliminate corporate greed by forcing corporations to pay much higher taxes.

Some People Incorrectly Believe Socialism Will Help to Eliminate Corporate Greed by Forcing Them to Pay Much Higher Taxes

One socialist assumption in the above criticism of capitalism is that all or most corporations are greedy. The second assumption is that the problem can be solved by forcing these companies to pay exorbitant taxes. Implicit in their arguments against corporations is that profits are inherently bad and foster greed, while taxes are essentially good because the resulting tax revenues go to the public sector.

Incidentally, this socialist rhetoric exemplifies how socialists get many people to follow socialism; they use force. In this case, it's the power that a socialist government has to force businesses to pay taxes at whatever level they deem appropriate.

It is worth pointing out that greed is a psychological human trait of people, who have a significant desire, or craving, or appetite for a material item such as food or money. Greed can also be a desire or lust for power and control over someone or something. Presumably, socialists are criticizing the management of corporations or the board of directors of corporations for seeking high profits, since corporations themselves don't have explicit human qualities.

It is also worth noting that socialists usually talk about raising taxes on corporations, but often fail to mention which specific tax or taxes they plan to impose or increase on companies. For example, corporate income taxes are assessed at the Federal and State levels and the associated income tax rates vary over time. Plus, corporations also pay a variety of additional taxes, such as payroll taxes, property taxes, sales taxes, and many other taxes. All told corporate taxes, even under capitalism, can be substantial.

Of course, because of the peculiarities in our complex tax laws, some companies can avoid paying taxes under some circumstances. The question arises why do some corporations appear to earn "book income" on their financial statements that are relatively positive and yet, not pay any income taxes at all?[240]

To answer this taxing question that perplexes many people, we need to understand that a corporation has a book income that follows Generally Accepted Accounting Principles (GAAP) issued by the Financial Accounting Standard Board (FASB). This is done to assure better "clarity, consistency, and comparability" in understanding financial statements.[241] At an overview level, book income is calculated by subtracting ordinary expenses and depreciation (of capital expenses) from revenues.[242]

It is important to note that only a portion of capital expenses are deducted, even though the company has paid out the full capital expense. GAAP standards produce a book income that can be considerably higher than the taxable net income which reflects the corporation's economic profit calculation after full expenses are deducted.[243]

So, it's possible that the book income of a corporation as reported in its annual financial statements will look reasonably high. It's also possible at the same time that the taxable net

137

income based on the economic profit calculation is low or even zero. In this instance, the corporation pays little or no income tax.

This apparent contradiction mirrors the tax policies that are embedded in the tax code. Yet, the tax policies are usually put in place with a purpose in mind, such as increasing job creation or spurring research investments.

Factors that influence whether or not a company can avoid paying income tax in a given year include:

- The nature, breakdown, and timing of the firm's expenses,
- The amount of capital expenses and the methods of depreciation used,
- If Net Operating Losses (NOL's), if any, are carried forward, and
- If foreign income is involved.[244]

Rather than treating profits as an avenue for allowing corporations to be greedy, it should be realized that profits with low or minimal or even zero taxes often happen as a result of government policy that has been formulated to enhance economic opportunity, growth, and prosperity.

For corporations, whose net taxable income is sufficiently high to generate taxes for the Federal and State treasuries, as many, if not most do, then the profits are a plus to the government and the public sector. They are one source of tax revenues to fund government programs.

Remember, all wealth created in an economy is produced in the private sector by businesses and individuals. No government organization can ever generate wealth in the public sector. Government revenues, if any, must be taxed away from the private sector.

It's been said:

> "You can't have people's needs met efficiently without profits."[245]

Pricing and profits work in tandem to identify customer needs and wants. They help identify what businesses, products, and services, consumers really need and want. They also signal to investors at all levels where scarce economic resources can best be deployed to meet unmet needs.

Failure to make a profit communicates the opposite message. A corporation or product line or service that loses money instead of making profits is telling the business world, the entrepreneurial risk-takers, and investors alike, stay away. This is a losing proposition. There is no consumer demand. The business, product or service is not important to customers. Work on different potential needs instead.

Finally, if corporations were to be taxed at outrageously high rates, the results would be awful for the economy. Corporations with insufficient profits left after taxes would have investors withdrawing money from the company by selling their common stocks. These same corporations could not invest in their own growth and certainly could not boost employment.

Most corporations pay a reasonably fair total tax chunk of money to the government, if you add up all the various tax liabilities they encounter.   Corporations that take advantage of tax breaks in the tax code that simultaneously stimulate economic opportunity, growth, and prosperity are entitled by public policy to those tax breaks.

Corporations are not greedy in general, and the market will deal harshly with corporations that do not serve consumers well. Raising taxes to exorbitantly high levels on corporations doesn't make sense economically for either the private sector or the public sector.

Now, let's turn our attention to a fourth argument socialists use to criticize capitalism, poverty. Socialists claim that they can help to eliminate poverty by providing all the basic needs that both citizens and non-citizens normally require.

Some People Incorrectly Believe Socialism Will Help to Eliminate Poverty by Providing All the Basic Needs of Both Citizens and Non-Citizens

This criticism of capitalism by socialists assumes that we know what poverty is in the real world. In fact, most people probably have some concept of poverty, but it likely differs quite a bit from person to person. Before addressing the question of whether or not socialism can eliminate poverty better than capitalism, let's think about the nature of poverty.

In life, there are two types of poverty: the "poverty of destitution" and the "poverty of comparison."[246] The poverty of destitution is a situation in which an individual can't meet their own basic physical needs for survival. The individual in poverty might not have adequate shelter or enough food to eat, for example. In contrast, the poverty of comparison is a different type of situation in which an individual doesn't have as many material possessions as some others do.

Such a person in today's America might live in a small apartment and have only one older car to drive. They probably are not able to afford a vacation to a tropical resort or many other luxury items. So, in comparison to others, who are better off financially, such a person might be said to be in a state of comparative poverty, but not in a state of destitute poverty because their basic survival needs are met adequately.

Certainly, a poor person living in America today lives a far better life than a poor person did in the year 750 AD or even in 1750 AD. In fact, it's possible that a poor person in America today lives a far better life than even a rich person did in the year 750 AD or in 1750 AD.

So, while the claim of socialists might be that they can eliminate poverty, just what kind of poverty are they trying to eliminate? It must be the poverty of comparison. After all, with about $1 Trillion dollars being spent by the U. S. government each year on over 90 different Federal, State, and local poverty programs[247] and additional dollars being donated by numerous private charitable organizations and millions of individuals, can anyone be suffering from the poverty of destitution in America today? Hopefully, we have eliminated the poverty of destitution already.

Another factor in the mix is how poverty is technically calculated. It can be confusing to some people. Currently, about 12% of Americans are considered to be living in poverty, yet, most welfare programs are not counted when determining the number of citizens in poverty. According to the Heritage Foundation:

> "Once cash, food and housing benefits are measured accurately the poverty rate falls from 12 to four percent."[248]

That's an incredible difference in poverty rates.

If some welfare programs continue not being counted for purposes of determining how many people live in poverty, higher poverty rates will continue to persist.

Consider another attempt to eliminate poverty, President Johnson's War on Poverty begun in the 1960's with its pledge to eliminate poverty in America. After over 50 years and $25 Trillion dollars spent, poverty still exists, even if accounting complexities make it challenging to determine an exact poverty rate in America.[249]

If anyone is suffering from the poverty of destitution in America, it is difficult to blame it on a lack of government spending. It's possible that some money is being gobbled up by waste, fraud, and corruption, however. But, that probably would take a massive effort to uncover completely.

Let's assume for the moment that the poverty rate is 4% in America today. After $25 Trillion dollars was spent on welfare programs for those in poverty, where did the $25 Trillion dollars come from? The answer is simple and straight forward. This large amount of wealth was provided by capitalism. This wealth was definitely not created by a socialist government running under socialism or communism.

So, it's absurd to think that if some socialists were successful in converting America from a Constitutional Republic to a socialist form of government, followed possibly by a communist country, that they could better eliminate poverty than the American Economy running under capitalism can do.

Socialists think that the economic growth and wealth created under capitalism will continue forever and will continue to fuel their socialist programs. Socialists don't realize that by destroying capitalism, as some want to do, they are cutting off the economic opportunity, growth, prosperity, and wealth they require to pay for any government programs, let alone poverty programs.

Instead of the poverty of destitution, if it's the poverty of comparison that socialists seek to eliminate, then they must want everyone to have the exact same income and the exact same level of wealth. This way there are no economic differences among people and no poverty of comparison. If this is the case, then the goal of eliminating poverty is really the same as the twin socialist goals previously discussed of eliminating inequality in income and eliminating inequality in wealth.

Of course, the result of achieving these twin goals will be for everyone to live in poverty, presumably at the exact same level of poverty (except, of course, for the socialist elites, who would live well). This makes sense since socialism always leads to spiritual, moral, and economic poverty (unless rescued in time by capitalism).

In America and in other nations, socialist thinking has not eliminated the poverty of destitution. Around the world, socialism has instead been the cause of much destitute poverty.

Incidentally, if socialism can't eliminate poverty among citizens in America, it surely can't also eliminate poverty among the non-citizens living in America too.

To summarize, socialism can't eliminate the poverty of destitution. Moreover, in seeking to eliminate the poverty of comparison, socialism is really pursuing the twin goals of the elimination of inequality in income and wealth. But, if socialism succeeds in reaching these two negative twin goals, it will create the poverty of destitution in the process.

Capitalism is not the cause of poverty. Socialism (in any of its various forms) is the cause of much poverty. Capitalism is best equipped to eliminate poverty. Socialism can't come even close to achieving the economic opportunity, growth, prosperity, and wealth of capitalism.

Now, let's turn our attention to a fifth argument socialists use to criticize capitalism, namely, socialists claim that socialism is more democratic than capitalism.

Some People Incorrectly Believe Socialism is More Democratic than Capitalism

It's a strange argument that socialists make when they believe that socialism is more democratic than capitalism. It's clearly false. But, let's explore some of the salient reasons why.

To begin with, the words "democratic" and "socialism" are fundamentally incompatible with one another.[250] In a democratic nation, while a majority vote determines the outcomes of free, fair, and honest elections for leaders and some issues submitted to the voters on the ballot, it can be said that the majority rules and the minority is protected.

In a socialist country that holds so-called democratic elections for leaders and issues, there are no comparable protections for the minority and their rights. In a socialist country, purported democratic elections can collapse into mob rule, with the freedoms of the minority trampled upon.

In a morality-based democracy, all of the nation's citizens implicitly choose to preserve, protect, and defend every other citizen's individual freedom. In America, freedom is an essential part of our Constitution, and this individual freedom has been respected by nearly all other citizens over our 240+ years of existence.

To illustrate how this point might or might not work in the future under potential socialist influence, suppose it's time for the citizens of America to elect a president and the two party major candidates running are respectively a populist conservative and a socialist.

Let's further assume in this example that the populist conservative wins the election. But, after the election, socialist supporters of the losing candidate shout down and publically berate any followers of the duly elected president and his populist conservative policies. In addition, let's say socialist professors and students ban conservative speakers, who support the president's policies, and cabinet-level secretaries, who work for the president, from speaking freely on university and college campuses.

In this illustration, socialists are squelching the free speech of political opponents or their followers. This is not consistent with a morality-based democracy.

In our Constitution, free speech is protected and America is a morality-based democracy. To learn more about the various elements of a morality-based democracy, please read my 2014 book: *Renewing America and Its Heritage of Freedom.*[251]

Another reason the words democratic and socialist don't work well together is that just like Venezuela, democratic socialism can quickly devolve from electing one socialist to office, to a dramatic shift in governments, to a totalitarian dictatorship. Lots of socialist efforts have begun with empty words that support democracy in theory and express a better life for workers in general, and then quickly morph into the elimination of individual freedom and economic deprivation.

Charles Cooke captured a succinct summary of democratic socialism by a proponent that shows why those two words don't fit well together:

"Ugo Okere, a self-described "democratic socialist" who ran for the Chicago City Council earlier this year, was recently praised in Jacobin magazine for explaining that "democratic socialism, to me, is about democratic control of every single facet of our life." That's one way of putting it, certainly. Another is "tyranny." Or, if you prefer, democratic tyranny."[252]

Certainly, socialism does not qualify as a form of democracy. It is too closely associated with tyranny and totalitarian dictatorship. At its very best, it limits freedom, and it can't be employed for long without damaging a country.

Capitalism, in sharp contrast, is closely related to democracy. The statement at the beginning of the section: "Some People Believe Socialism is More Democratic than Capitalism" is patently false. Instead, capitalism is more democratic than socialism.

Now, let's turn our attention to a sixth argument socialists use to criticize capitalism, namely, socialists claim that socialism is more moral than capitalism.

Some People Incorrectly Believe Socialism is More Moral than Capitalism

Socialists think that because capitalism is so incredibly successful economically and results in so much economic growth and prosperity, somehow capitalism must be materialistic, foster greed, and has little interest in helping those less fortunate. Nothing can be farther from the truth. Earlier, we have addressed the assertion that corporations under capitalism are greedy and have dismissed that argument as untrue. Let's present a moral case for capitalism, and show that indeed capitalism is more moral than socialism.

Without question, from an economic perspective, capitalism beats socialism hands down. Even Karl Marx and Friedrich Engels in the *Communist Manifesto* acknowledged the productive forces of capitalism in these words:

> "The bourgeoisie, during its rule of scarce 100 years, has created more massive and more colossal productive forces than have all preceding generations together."[253]

Yet, this much heralded economic efficiency that has lifted the standard of living for millions of people around the world is not nearly the only reason capitalism is far superior to socialism morally. Indeed, capitalism thrives on human peace and freedom.[254]

Morality and freedom are inherent principles in capitalism, arising out of our Judeo-Christian heritage and standing in stark contrast to the development of socialism from its immoral roots in atheism and secularism. Socialism ignores moral principles when they impose socialist ideology on its citizens against their will. Socialism also destroys individual freedom when it gets in the way of socialist and communist objectives.

Personal property ownership, the Rule of Law, and the enforcement of contracts all enhance human dignity and support voluntary transactions in a free market.[255] Socialism, either initially or eventually, and almost always inevitably, leads to the use of force.

Because socialism violates human nature, it often requires some type of force to compel the results it seeks. Socialism usually involves centralized planning enforced with harsh controls, coercion, compulsion and sometimes even violence.

Capitalism is more moral than socialism by virtue of the fact that it fosters voluntary, mutually beneficial, and peaceful transactions. It doesn't permit, and it definitely doesn't require, force or violence to achieve action.[256]

Incidentally, capitalism lends itself not only to peace within a nation, but also among various nations. Free and fair trade makes global cooperation voluntary, mutually beneficial, and peaceful as well.

Socialism has a long history of fomenting revolution, bloody violence, and civil war among socialist factions in differing countries.

Once again, capitalism is more moral that socialism in the global arena and in the peaceful interaction of nations.

Let's make another point. Some people perceive capitalism as materialistic and therefore they think socialism is more moral than capitalism. Let's think about this bogus charge.

Capitalism provides the tools to create economic efficiency, opportunity, growth, and prosperity. It doesn't indicate to citizens how much money or wealth a person needs. Materialism is a value that some citizens might choose to pursue. Many other citizens don't share that particular value and will live differently. Materialism is not a criticism of capitalism by its very nature; rather, it's a critique of an individual's personal values and lifestyle.[257]

Another moral plus for capitalism is that it is the most humane method to allow individuals to be themselves, despite the vast array of characteristics, interests, tastes, beliefs, talents, needs, and wants they exhibit in life. Socialism makes the inhumane decision and policy rule to treat everyone, not as individuals with unique needs, but rather as monolithic, robotic commodities.

Capitalism is more moral than socialism because:

- Capitalism provides better management in the production and distribution of scarce economic resources,
- Capitalism provides more citizens with the benefits of economic opportunity, growth, prosperity, and wealth, and
- Capitalism continues to raise the standard of living for nations employing its principles,
- Capitalism includes morality and freedom arising out of its Judeo-Christian heritage as part of its inherent principles,
- Capitalism supports liberty and democracy,
- Capitalism includes personal property ownership, the Rule of Law, and the enforcement of contracts that enhance human dignity,
- Capitalism supports voluntary cooperation, mutually beneficial, and peaceful transactions in a free market,

- Capitalism avoids the use of centralized planning, harsh controls, coercion, compulsion, and violence,
- Capitalism lends itself not only to peace within a nation, but also peace among various nations,
- Capitalism lends itself to free and fair trade making global cooperation voluntary, mutually beneficial, and peaceful,
- Capitalism doesn't foment revolution, bloody violence, and civil war around the world,
- Capitalism doesn't require citizens to choose a lifestyle of materialism, and
- Capitalism is the most humane method to allow individuals to express themselves and to live the lifestyle they choose.

For all of these reasons and more, capitalism is more moral than socialism.

Looking at both the arguments some people level against capitalism and the realities of capitalism versus socialism, it is clear the capitalism is far superior to socialism in a moral sense.

This chapter answered the question: Why do some people find socialism so appealing and seductive when the evidence indicates capitalism is a much better system?

Let's next turn our attention to some additional reasons why some people find capitalism superior to socialism.

Chapter 7

What Are Additional Reasons Some People Believe Capitalism is Superior to Socialism?

In the previous chapters, we have seen many reasons why capitalism is far superior to socialism in theory and in practice. We have also studied some of the main reasons socialists argue in favor of socialism and have found their reasoning to be faulty. Let's next look at some additional reasons that some people prefer capitalism to socialism.

Some People Think Capitalism Encourages Citizens to be More Creative

Creativity is both a subtle reason in favor of capitalism over socialism and a reason that is often neglected. But, it is an important justification for capitalism over socialism. If we look at nations over the decades and centuries, it is clear that countries can suffer from both material poverty and spiritual and moral poverty. In particular, this spiritual and moral poverty can take the form of a discouraged or depressed human spirit. The ambience and mood of a nation can be stifling and suffocating, and can partially threaten or completely curtail creativity.

Creativity implies new ideas, new ways of doing things, and sometimes "change" in some aspect of our lives. Authors Austin Hill and Scott Rae capture the significance of creativity within capitalism in these words:

> "At the center of the capitalist economic system is the elevation of human creativity ... capitalism not only affirms and encourages human creativity, it relies upon it as well ... A society needs at least some of its members to continually be discovering better ways of accomplishing the established tasks, while at the same time developing new tasks ... Without such individuals, an economic system stagnates, and the broader society suffers."[258]

Recall political economist Joseph A. Schumpeter's description of the dynamic nature of capitalism with the phrase "Creative Destruction." It's true with capitalism that while some businesses are being destroyed, other new businesses are constantly being created. Consider the evolution of telephones, from the black desktop rotary phones of old, to the colorful touchtone phones, to the cell phones that flipped open, to the smart phones used today for a myriad of personal apps, such as displaying your boarding pass at the airport gate.

Capitalism is designed to support and encourage creativity in the economy. Closely related to creativity is innovation, another reason some people think capitalism is superior to socialism.

Some People Think Capitalism Encourages Citizens to Develop More Innovative Businesses, Business Models, Products, and Services

With creativity usually come some forms of innovation. Innovation can take many different shapes and forms, many different patterns and functions. Take our smart phone illustration once again. A creative entrepreneur might design a powerful new app for aggregating the news by industry for our smart phones.

Certainly, innovation can take other forms besides a new phone app. Innovation might result in a new product or service, or even a new business model, a new business, or an entirely new industry. In capitalism, ideas that are deemed worthy and likely to succeed in the marketplace will typically find family and friends to help launch the idea, with angel investors and venture capitalists nearby searching for new businesses to invest in all the time.

The incentive for both creativity and innovation in capitalism is the sense of accomplishment of creating something from scratch that is worthwhile. For example, pharmaceutical research scientists work tirelessly to find new cures that will prolong life for patients with a serious illness or will cure a disease outright.

Socialists often criticize the pharmaceutical companies for their high drug prices, not realizing the billions of dollars of research and development (R&D) costs that are required to find a new drug, test it adequately, and put it through the necessary steps to get approval by the FDA for safe general use.

Some immunotherapy treatments can cost in the hundreds of thousands of dollars per treatment. Without the incentives of capitalism to find creative and innovative new treatments and the ability to recoup the initial R&D costs, immunotherapy drugs would likely not be available today to help patients.

In addition to creativity and innovation, another reason some people think capitalism is superior to socialism is that capitalism empowers greater morality and freedom in a nation.

Some People Think Capitalism Empowers Greater Morality and Freedom in a Nation

Our Judeo-Christian heritage forms a solid foundation for our faith in God. In turn, our belief in God empowers our belief in the human dignity that we all share together as children of God. From this human dignity, it follows that individuals have both freedom and morality in their spiritual DNA.

Capitalism utilizes morality and freedom as two of its inherent principles. Indeed, we know that morality and freedom are integral components of the Architecture of American Capitalism that I discussed in an earlier book.[259]

Socialism's lineage, in sharp contrast to capitalism, is based on atheism and secularism. Its dreary and bleak heritage is devoid of a robust system of morality and freedom. So, it's no wonder that socialism fails so miserably in practice.

Capitalism would never permit the determined and deliberate torture and murder of its citizens for reasons of implementing a centralized and planned economy. It also would not oversee a cold-blooded famine, starving its citizen to enforce calculated socialist objectives.

Thus, capitalism naturally empowers greater morality and freedom than socialism in nations that embrace capitalism as its cultural, political, and economic system.

Another plus for capitalism over socialism is in the area of charitable giving. Let's look at that topic next.

Some People Think Capitalism Encourages More Charitable Giving than Socialism

Capitalism has a track record of charitable generosity. According to one source:

> "... Jennifer Baker and Mark White note a strong correlation between how market-oriented a society is and how likely its members are to volunteer and contribute money to charity. People who live in robust market economies, such as the United States, are more generous towards the less well-off than people in countries with less developed markets."[260]

Why might this be the case?

For one thing, because capitalism is closely associated with our Judeo-Christian heritage, a capitalist nation with many religious citizens might be expected to be more charitable than a socialist country where atheism is more prevalent.[261]

We know that people who attend religious services are more likely to donate to religious organizations. But, in addition, they are also more likely to donate to secular groups as well. Another likely factor is simply that donating to charities is a basic belief of many religious groups.[262]

Let's look at a little more research before leaving this topic. According to the World Giving Index, associated with the Charities Aid Foundation in the United Kingdom, and based on the Gallup's World Poll surveys of 1.3 million people, among 128 countries:

> "The United States has been the most generous country in the world over the past decade."[263]

Note that this research didn't measure total charitable donations by dollars or other monetary units, but rather by percent of people answering "Yes" to three questions dealing with charitable generosity.

Once again, capitalism in America ranked as more generous than other socialist countries. It seems fair to conclude that capitalism encourages more charitable giving than socialism.

Still another avenue for comparison between capitalism and socialism is personal initiative and responsibility.

Some People Think Capitalism Encourages Citizens to Take More Personal Initiative and Responsibility

To understand how capitalism encourages and supports personal initiative and responsibility, it's helpful to look back to the medieval ages in Europe and England when capitalism first influenced economic reality.

Back then, and actually for a period of a few centuries, England was essentially a feudalist culture. There was no middle class. The "haves" were the lords and the "have nots" were the serfs. All the resources were owned by the lords. The serfs had no hope of moving beyond their poor serfdom status. These fiefdoms run by lords existed as virtually independent states within the larger nation of England led by a king or queen and a Parliament.[264]

When competition first entered the picture from outside the fiefdoms, locally grown agricultural crops began to be inadequate. Bad weather (probably not from climate change), famines, and plagues, also weighed heavily on agricultural production. Warfare among the lords ensued.[265]

Philosophers, such as Adam Smith, influenced many citizens directly or indirectly with their early capitalist ideas including:

- Warfare doesn't lead to economic growth and prosperity;
- Rather, warfare leads to draining economic resources from a nation;
- Independent citizens and serfs must be free to charge for their labor and skills from whomever they wish to work; and
- Citizens free to pursue their own self-interest will enrich a nation with abundance and prosperity.[266]

Closely tied to this capitalist thinking were the twin concepts of personal initiative and responsibility that eventually emerged throughout most free market economies.

Indeed, personal initiative and responsibility were ultimately in the hands of each individual citizen. It was not a citizen's neighbor, or the lord, or the king or queen, or the Parliament, or any government entity that must show primary initiative and responsibility for the average citizen.

Of course, there were always exceptions to complete self-reliance, including orphans, widows, the ill, and the elderly.

With socialism, of course, comes socialist thinking that citizens are all victims and must be cared for by the State throughout their lives. That's the basis for free everything that socialist rhetoric often promises, but rarely delivers to its citizens.

Clearly, from its very origins, both personal initiative and responsibility are built into capitalism and capitalism encourages and supports personal initiative and responsibility.

Capitalism also offers another favorable comparison with socialism. Capitalism encourages citizens to be more cooperative in the workplace and around the nation.

Some People Think Capitalism Encourages Citizens to be More Cooperative in the Workplace and Around the Nation

Capitalism engenders a spirit of cooperation in citizens that impacts the workplace and the entire nation. Why is this fact the case?

Capitalism requires cooperation among players in the marketplace – customers and business people – in order to accomplish an objective. Usually, the objective is to design, develop, manufacture (or provide), market, and deliver a particular product or service that meets someone's needs.

Without cooperation and teamwork, a product or service can't come to market in the first place. Without the help of marketing and sales people and sometimes advertising experts and others, a potential customer might not even be aware that a given product or service exists in the marketplace. Cooperation and teamwork are also necessary to help a customer know if the product or service is right for their needs. Finally, delivery and installation people might need to work together to place the product in service for the customer.

A business within a capitalist economy is one team banding together to serve customers. The marketplace is an even larger team of multiple businesses, products, and services communicating with customers to meet numerous needs in parallel.

In capitalism, businesses or individual contributors within businesses (employees) that choose not to cooperate, or choose not to be civil, or choose not to communicate, with customers, will find that there is a financial price to be paid. Businesses that act badly will lose customers and will risk bankruptcy. Employees, who don't cooperate or don't serve customers well, might lose their jobs.

Incidentally, a potential employee can be thought of as an "individual personal company." That person might go to college to enhance their skills. Then, they might develop a catchy, well-written resume with visual appeal to market themselves to potential employers. They might also practice interviewing to get a good job with a business.

All along the route from personal education to employment, the potential employee (and then the actual employee) is his or her own "individual personal company." Plus, some people choose not to get a permanent employer at all, but prefer being self-employed on an on-going basis.

In capitalism, citizens are free to pursue the best way to meet their financial needs. But, whatever method they choose, it will of necessity involve cooperation.

Cooperation in capitalism actually spans markets that cross State and local geographical boundaries. We can see then that the same type of cooperation that capitalism spawns in a local market actually can reach across the entire nation.

How about markets that are global in nature? Does capitalism's influence extend past a nation's markets and impact free and fair trade as well as both cooperation and peace among many nations?

Some People Think Capitalism Encourages Free and Fair Trade and More Cooperation and Peace among Nations

It's also true that capitalism not only encourages and supports voluntary, mutually beneficial, and cooperative transactions within a given market and within a particular nation, but capitalism also encourages and supports voluntary, mutually beneficial, and cooperative transactions among those nations that participate in free and fair trade.

Similar to a free market, free and fair trade and the corresponding cooperative and peaceful exchanges that result, benefit all nations at the same time. Free trade is actually an extension of a free market with the major practical difference that the geographical boundaries of the marketplace go beyond the borders of any one nation. Currency differences and exchanges might also factor into the transactions.

Johan Norberg captures some of the benefits of free trade in these words:

> "Free trade is primarily a good thing because it brings freedom: freedom for people to buy what they want from whoever they please, but also to sell to whoever wants to buy. As an added economic benefit, this freedom leads to the efficient use of resources and capital."[267]

Free and fair trade is win-win. It is not win-lose and it is not lose-lose. All nations in such a transaction normally win.

Before leaving the topic of free and fair trade, one other essential point must be made that is likely not self-evident. Free and fair trade is not only beneficial because it significantly contributes to economic growth and prosperity, but it is also particularly essential for creating and maintaining peace among nations.[268] How can free and fair trade help to create more peace among nations?

As we mentioned before, free and fair trade is a voluntary exchange that is peaceful in nature. Free and fair trade generally happens without force, without threats, without coercion, without compulsion, without violence, and without warfare, of any sort. Free and fair trade takes place because both parties gain economic value in this peaceful, voluntary process.

Just think about the opposite of a peaceful transaction in a free market or in a free trade situation. For example, does a company in San Diego go to war with another company in Los Angeles over a contract dispute? Does a consumer in Atlanta go to battle with a consumer in Miami over an internet purchase gone awry? Of course, they don't.

Companies don't go to war with each other in America and neither do consumers. It's unthinkable. Then, why does war make sense for any government, anywhere in the world? It's certainly not constructive in any way imaginable. It's fundamentally a destructive process as Adam Smith thought.

With capitalism among free nations, nations also realize that peaceful and voluntary cooperation is far superior to violence and warfare to boost their economies.

Free and fair trade mirrors free markets as a peaceful, voluntary, and cooperative process, but these exchanges link nations together, rather than simply companies and consumers. Those nations that work together don't want to wage war against each other, because their peaceful, voluntary, and cooperative economic exchanges yield much greater economic value for all the nations involved.

If we had capitalism, including free and fair trade around the world, we would likely finally achieve the dream of world peace (and prosperity too).

Capitalism with its inherent principles of freedom and morality are the true foundations of cooperation and global peace. Free and fair trade contributes mightily to both of these true foundations of global peace.

We can see that capitalism by its nature not only empowers free and fair trade, but it also encourages more cooperation and peace among nations than does socialism.

In the previous chapters, we have seen many reasons why capitalism is far superior to socialism in theory and in practice. We have also studied some of the main reasons socialists argue in favor of socialism and have found their reasoning to be faulty. Finally, in this chapter, we have looked at a number of additional reasons some people think that capitalism is far more preferable than socialism.

Let's next look at some other reasons that some people believe socialism is inferior to capitalism.

Chapter 8

What Are Other Reasons Some People Believe Socialism is Inferior to Capitalism?

Besides the many reasons we have seen that indicate that capitalism is far superior to socialism, there are actually quite a few other reasons why some people specifically reject socialism. In these instances, some people believe socialism is completely inferior to capitalism. Let's look at these ideas next.

Some People Think that Socialism Can't Really Deliver on All Those Grandiose Promises that They Sometimes Make

Socialists are often notorious for making big promises that appear like pie-in-the-sky dreams and that carry enormous price tags. In reality, socialists have no way of paying for these pipe dreams, despite raising taxes to tremendously high levels, confiscating private property, and nationalizing industries.

In the real world, there is a finite limit to the wealth of a nation. It is produced and contained within the private sector and a socialist government can't tax away more than 100% of the wealth in the private sector. Recall too, in the public sector, no wealth can be created, only consumed.

That's why some people think that socialism can't really deliver on all those grandiose promises that they sometimes make to citizens.

Some People Think that Socialism Will Result in Living with a Lot More Taxes, a Lot More Regulations, and a Lot More Inflation

Part and parcel of much socialist thinking is the necessity to raise taxes to nose-bleed levels to finance their gargantuan government programs and their concomitant government waste and corruption that repeatedly occurs after a huge bureaucracy is created.

In parallel with increasing tax rates on most citizens to steep levels, the economy is typically constrained with burdensome regulations and monetary policies that generate value-diminishing inflation. Citizens usually suffer under socialism.

It's not surprising then that some people reject socialism because in their clear thinking they believe socialism will result in a lot more taxes, a lot more regulations, and a lot more inflation.

Some People Think Socialism Will Result in Living with a Lot Less Healthcare Services and Healthcare Innovation

In addition, some pragmatic people consider socialism inferior to capitalism for one other special reason. They are concerned with their healthcare – both their current healthcare and healthcare innovation in the future. Why?

It's been said that if you have your health, you have everything. To some extent, that statement is probably true.

For some people, healthcare is of paramount importance. They want good healthcare and they want it when it's needed. They don't want to wait six months for an urgent surgery to take place. They certainly don't want to die, while waiting for a much needed healthcare procedure or test.

They also know that newer innovations in healthcare might be of future life-saving value to themselves and their families. They want the pipeline of healthcare and pharmaceutical innovations to continue unabated. They want the competition, innovation, and progress that capitalism offers the healthcare industry to remain intact. They see socialism as shutting down this innovation channel to everyone's detriment.

Universal healthcare, single-payer healthcare, socialized medicine, free healthcare for all, or whatever term socialists might use to describe it, is still a centrally planned government healthcare bureaucracy that will most likely result in acute shortages, rationing of healthcare products and services, as well as the virtual elimination of healthcare and pharmaceutical innovations.

That's the dismal track record of single-payer healthcare around the world where it has been tried.[269]

It is easy to understand why some people think socialism will result in living with a lot less healthcare services and healthcare innovation.

Some People Think Socialism Will Result in Living with a Lot Less Energy Resources at Much Higher Prices

Another rationale for people rejecting socialism in favor of capitalism deals with energy independence, availability, and prices.

Socialist rhetoric frequently admonishes citizens to cut back on energy to "save" the planet from so-called "climate change," which is disputed by many scientists and engineers.[270] In fact, some people believe that climate change arguments are made by socialists in an attempt to control one of the most vital industries in America – the energy industry. Controlling America's energy industry would, in essence, control the American Economy.

Rather than cutback on energy resources entirely, some socialists might prefer to raises taxes on energy or severely restrict its usage. Such taxes, regulations, and restrictions would have the effect of reducing America's standard of living, economic growth, and prosperity. Plus, you can reasonably expect energy prices to skyrocket in the process.

According to the U.S. Energy Information Administration (EIA), America became a net exporter of energy for the first time in its history in September 2019. That means generally that our economy is not only energy independent of foreign energy sources, but it is also responsible for suppling energy overseas to others as well.

According to Oilprice.com:

> "Just a decade ago, the U.S. was importing 10 million bpd more crude oil and petroleum products than it was exporting."[271]

That's 10 million barrels per day (bpd) imported by the U.S. from up to 37 foreign sources of crude oil per month. At the same time, America's oil exports were primarily restricted to Canada.[272]

This turnaround from U. S. net energy importer to net energy exporter is likely directly attributable to limiting regulations and restrictions on energy exploration and production. This is one more illustration of the benefits of economic freedom.

It's no wonder then some people reject socialism and prefer capitalism. They realistically think socialism would result in living with a lot less energy resources at much higher prices.

Some People Think Socialism Will Result in a Much Lower Standard of Living

Given all the points made above, it's not a stretch for some people to expect a reduced standard of living under socialism. Higher taxes, fiscal irresponsibility, more regulations, weaker dollar, and increased inflation all point directly toward a declining standard of living.

Reductions in healthcare services and innovation as well as fewer energy resources at higher prices also point to a decrease in the standard of living under socialism.

Closely related to this lower standard of living under socialism, GDP growth will likely drop precipitously, and economic opportunity, growth, prosperity, and wealth will fall as well.

It makes sense that some people prefer capitalism over socialism because they want their standard of living to increase, year-over-year, and certainly not decrease.

Some People Think Socialism Will Unleash on America – Spiritual, Moral, and Economic Bankruptcy

Socialism as we have seen earlier fundamentally violates human nature. It also advocates and works tirelessly for limiting or eliminating individual human freedom and liberty. On top of these terrible factors, socialism rejects basic morality in place of its own ad hoc immorality that gives it maximum control over its citizens.

Socialism can't help but move a country toward spiritual, moral, and economic bankruptcy. The only questions deal with "how fast" the move toward spiritual, moral, and economic bankruptcy will take place, and if a country will recognize its errors "in time" and will bring in capitalism, freedom, and morality to save the country from it probable fate.

Some people much prefer capitalism over socialism because they believe socialism will unleash spiritual, moral, and economic bankruptcy on America.

Some People Think Socialism Will Result in Destroying America – Our Constitution, the Rule of Law, Our Morality, Freedom, Peace, and Prosperity

If socialism were to be chosen as a new American political and economic system of government by one or more elections, or by some evolutionary process of eroding our freedoms and relinquishing control to the government, or by a revolution as some have radically advocated, some people think socialism will destroy America.

If it were ever to take over power in America, some people think socialism (and potentially a communist totalitarian dictatorship) will result in destroying America's wonderful 240+ year Constitutional Republic, along with our Constitution, the Rule of Law, and our morality, individual liberty and freedom, as well as our peace and prosperity.

Some socialists think that socialism can exist within our Constitutional Republic, but that is not the case. Just as many socialists are attempting to curtail our Freedom of Speech and our freedom to keep and bear arms, socialism would most likely result in continued encroachments on all our liberties. Also, socialists, for example, can't expect a weak private sector to fund their hefty, inordinately expensive, and grandiose promises of freebies for citizens and non-citizens alike.

With socialism, Americans can't expect equality under the Rule of Law when so many on the Left want to have two competing systems of justice – one for the socialist elites, and one for regular citizens.

It is completely understandable that some people think socialism will result in destroying America – our Constitution, the Rule of Law, our morality, freedom, peace, and prosperity. No wonder these people reject socialism and believe capitalism is far superior to socialism.

In the previous chapters, we have seen many reasons why capitalism is far superior to socialism in theory and in practice. We have also studied some of the main reasons socialists argue in favor of socialism and have found their reasoning to be faulty. Moreover, we have looked at a number of additional reasons some people think that capitalism is far more preferable than socialism. Plus, we have reviewed why some people think socialism to be inferior to capitalism. Thus, we have looked at socialism from many different and distinct vantage points.

In the final chapter, let's summarize the world of differences between capitalism and socialism.

Chapter 9

Real World Capitalism vs. Real World Socialism – A World of Difference!

Capitalism and socialism can't be farther apart than they are in the real world. In theory and in practice, they are polar opposites and generate diametrically conflicting results. The comparisons between capitalism and socialism are stark and in sharp contrast in every dimension imaginable.

Real World Capitalism

Citizens that choose capitalism over socialism make a profoundly upbeat and positive decision that resonates over their religious, cultural, intellectual, political, and economic lives in surprisingly valuable ways for generations.

With capitalism come these powerful, life-giving, and life-affirming benefits:

- A peaceful and stable religious, cultural, intellectual, political, and economic civilization that is based on our Judeo-Christian heritage, morality, and the Freedom of religion,
- A peaceful and stable family heritage that provides for the traditional family structures of our Judeo-Christian heritage – family, marriage, life, and sexual identities,

- A peaceful and stable political heritage based on our Constitution and its guarantees of individual liberty and freedom,
- A peaceful and stable justice system based on our Constitution and equality under the Rule of Law,
- A peaceful and stable economic system based on our Constitution and our economic freedom, and
- A peaceful and stable economy that promotes and creates economic opportunity, growth, innovation, prosperity, and wealth creation.

Real World Socialism

Citizens seduced by the bogus rhetoric and false promises of socialism can expect:

- To endure life with an atheistic, pseudo religion, that foregoes morality when it's convenient for the socialist elite,
- To endure life without the traditional and stable family structures of civilization – family, marriage, life, and sexual identities,
- To endure life within an immoral culture,
- To endure a life with a cold-hearted, centrally planned, bureaucratic, corrupt, and authoritarian government,
- To endure a life without nearly all liberty and freedom that Americans have taken for granted for over two centuries,

- To endure life without the Rule of Law – one justice system for socialist elites and one justice system for regular citizens,
- To endure a life without economic opportunity, growth, innovation, prosperity, and wealth creation,
- To endure a life with a stagnate economy, characterized by shortages, rationing, long and frustrating waiting lines, and high inflation,
- To endure a life with poverty, suffering, and destitution, and
- Possibly, in some cases, to endure a life with family and friends that are tortured and murdered at the whim of a totalitarian and dictatorial government.

Socialists lament and make excuses for those horrible examples of failed socialist and communist countries that have created untold poverty and destitution. Some socialists even want to overlook the millions and millions of deaths under socialism as regrettable. Supposedly, Marxism wasn't followed properly in all these many and varied instances.

Socialism begins in atheism and seeks the abolition of religion, morality, the family, private property, and individual freedom. It also seeks revolution or in some cases evolution as the means toward their ends.

It's time to get real and move civilization forward.

Socialism doesn't work. Let's stop wasting time, energy, emotions, and dollars over a utopian idea that is clearly a proven and colossal failure.

Ronald Reagan is quoted as saying about socialism that:

> "Socialism only works in two places: Heaven where they don't need it and hell where they already have it."[273]

A World of Difference!

In truth, there is a world of difference between real world capitalism and real world socialism.

Capitalism begins in our Judeo-Christian heritage with the inherent and vital principles of freedom and morality.

In the Bible, we learn:

> "Now the Lord is the Spirit, and where the Spirit of the Lord is, there is freedom."[274]

Truly, God abides in freedom. In His infinite love and perfection, God freely chose to create man to share with man His blessed life.

Built upon that heritage is a marvelous set of founding documents that are a model for the world.

The Declaration of Independence, America's founding document, declared America as a free and independent nation, and articulated the nation's moral vision. Consider these fundamental words:

> "WE hold these Truths to be self-evident, that all Men are created equal, that they are endowed by their

Creator with certain unalienable Rights, that among these are Life, Liberty, and the Pursuit of Happiness ..."

As Thomas Jefferson has said:

"The God who gave us life gave us liberty at the same time ..."[275]

In addition, our Constitution, America's political framework and guardian of our liberty, begins with these critical words:

"We the People of the United States, in Order to form a more perfect Union, establish Justice, insure domestic Tranquility, provide for the common defence, promote the general Welfare, and secure the Blessings of Liberty to ourselves and our Posterity, do ordain and establish this Constitution for the United States of America."

Capitalism is all about freedom and prosperity. Capitalism has created the most economic wealth and highest standard of living in the world. It has also overseen the development of some of the greatest technological, healthcare, and pharmaceutical innovations in the world. Plus, over the years, capitalism has also provided more economic help to nations torn by war, disease, and disaster than any other nation in the history of civilization.

Real world capitalism is far superior to real world socialism.

About the Author

Gerard F. Lameiro Ph.D. is an author, political analyst, and expert on forecast models. Dr. Lameiro is the author of six books and is a popular TV and Talk Radio show personality that does up to about 500 media interviews a year. Dr. Lameiro has been called by media hosts "America's #1 Political Analyst" and the "Nostradamus of Political Elections."

Dr. Lameiro accurately and consistently predicted a Trump victory long before most pollsters and pundits gave Trump even a small chance of winning the presidential election. Dr. Lameiro correctly predicted every State that candidate Trump actually carried in the 2016 election, including Florida, Pennsylvania, Ohio, Michigan, and Wisconsin.

Dr. Lameiro has worked on many political campaigns in various roles, including Ronald Reagan's 1976 and 1980 presidential election campaigns. Dr. Lameiro was a member of the 1980 Presidential Electoral College and personally cast one electoral vote for Ronald Reagan for President of the United States of America.

Other Books by the Author

- More Great News for America (2018)
- Great News for America (2016)
- Renewing America and Its Heritage of Freedom (2014)
- Choosing the Good Life (2010)
- America's Economic War (2009)

Notes

[1] Joshua Muravchik, Heaven on Earth: The Rise, Fall, and Afterlife of Socialism (New York: Encounter Books, 2002, 2003, 2019), pp. 57 – 93, pp. 147 – 175, pp. 335 – 360.

[2] Thomas J. DiLorenzo, *The Problem with Socialism* (Washington, DC: Regnery Publishing, 2016), pp. 77 – 83.

[3] Thomas J. DiLorenzo, *The Problem with Socialism* (Washington, DC: Regnery Publishing, 2016), pp. 77 – 83.

[4] Thomas J. DiLorenzo, *The Problem with Socialism* (Washington, DC: Regnery Publishing, 2016), pp. 77 – 83.

[5] Thomas J. DiLorenzo, *The Problem with Socialism* (Washington, DC: Regnery Publishing, 2016), pp. 77 – 83.

[6] Thomas J. DiLorenzo, *The Problem with Socialism* (Washington, DC: Regnery Publishing, 2016), pp. 77 – 83.

[7] Please see, for example, Ernest Belfort Bax, *The Religion of Socialism* (Freeport, NY: Books for Libraries Press, 1972), pp. 52 – 53. The quote is cited in: Joshua Muravchik, Heaven on Earth: The Rise, Fall, and Afterlife of Socialism (New York: Encounter Books, 2002, 2003, 2019), p. 358.

[8] "Short History of the Battle Over the Ten Commandments in Alabama," WSFA 12 News (Montgomery, AL: WSFA 12 News, August 1, 2001), https://www.wsfa.com/story/421482/short-history-of-the-battle-over-the-ten-commandments-in-alabama/ .

[9] Jonathan Stempel, "U.S. court rejects atheists' appeal over 'In God We Trust' on money," Reuters, August 28, 2018, https://www.reuters.com/article/us-usa-religion-motto/us-court-rejects-atheists-appeal-over-in-god-we-trust-on-money-idUSKCN1LD24K .

[10] For a more in-depth understanding of individual freedom, morality, and its relationship to God, please see: Gerard Francis Lameiro, *Renewing America and Its Heritage of*

Freedom: What Freedom-Loving Americans Can Do to Help
(Fort Collins, CO: Gerard Francis Lameiro, 2014), pp. 7 – 35.

[11] For a more in-depth discussion of Eternal Law, Divine Law, Natural Law, and Human Law, please see: Gerard Francis Lameiro, *Renewing America and Its Heritage of Freedom: What Freedom-Loving Americans Can Do to Help* (Fort Collins, CO: Gerard Francis Lameiro, 2014), pp. 29 – 35.

[12] For example, consider the anti-Jewish statements of Karl Marx. Please see, for example: Joshua Muravchik, Heaven on Earth: The Rise, Fall, and Afterlife of Socialism (New York: Encounter Books, 2002, 2003, 2019), pp. 63 – 76.

[13] Joshua Muravchik, Heaven on Earth: The Rise, Fall, and Afterlife of Socialism (New York: Encounter Books, 2002, 2003, 2019), pp. 358.

[14] Anna North, "The controversy around Virginia's new abortion bill, explained," Vox.com, February 1, 2019, https://www.vox.com/2019/2/1/18205428/virginia-abortion-bill-kathy-tran-ralph-northam .

[15] Sally C. Pipes, *The False Promise of Single-Payer Health Care* (New York: Encounter Books, 2018).

[16] Joshua Muravchik, Heaven on Earth: The Rise, Fall, and Afterlife of Socialism (New York: Encounter Books, 2002, 2003, 2019), pp. 273 – 312.

[17] David Satter, "100 Years of Communism—and 100 Million Dead," The Wall Street Journal, November 6, 2017, https://www.wsj.com/articles/100-years-of-communismand-100-million-dead-1510011810 .

[18] Marion Smith, "Education Is Socialism's Only Antidote," *National Review,* May 17, 2019, https://www.nationalreview.com/2019/05/education-socialisms-only-antidote/ .

[19] Greg Ip, Venezuela's Collapse Exposes the Fake Socialism Debated in U.S., *The Wall Street Journal,* February 6, 2019, https://www.wsj.com/articles/venezuelas-collapse-exposes-the-fake-socialism-debated-in-u-s-11549465200 .

[20] Greg Ip, Venezuela's Collapse Exposes the Fake Socialism Debated in U.S., *The Wall Street Journal,* February 6, 2019, https://www.wsj.com/articles/venezuelas-collapse-exposes-the-fake-socialism-debated-in-u-s-11549465200

[21] Kevin D. Williamson, *The Politically Incorrect Guide® to Socialism* (Washington, DC: Regnery Publishing, A Salem Communications Company, 2011), pp. 147 – 169.

[22] Nick Kangadis, "The Average Venezuelan Lost 24 Pounds Last Year From Hunger, Study Finds," Media Research Center, February 23, 2018, https://www.mrctv.org/blog/university-study-reports-90-pct-venezuela-poverty-people-losing-significant-weight .

[23] Justin T. Haskins, *Socialism is Evil* (Boston: Justin Hawkins and The Henry Dearborn Institute for Liberty, 2018), 27 – 38.

[24] Justin T. Haskins, *Socialism is Evil* (Boston: Justin Hawkins and The Henry Dearborn Institute for Liberty, 2018), 27 – 38.

[25] Allan Bloom, *The Republic of Plato, Second Edition, Translated with Notes and an Interpretive Essay by Allan Bloom* (New York: Basic Books, 1969, 1991).

[26] Mark R. Levin, *Ameritopia: The Unmaking of America* (New York: threshold Editions, a Division of Simon & Schuster, Inc., 2012), p. 33.

[27] Mark R. Levin, *Ameritopia: The Unmaking of America* (New York: threshold Editions, a Division of Simon & Schuster, Inc., 2012), pp. 23 – 36.

[28] Frederick Copleston, S.J., *A History of Philosophy: Volume I: Greece and Rome from the Pre-Socratics to Plotinus* (New York: Image Books, Doubleday, 1946), pp. 225 – 233.

[29] Mark R. Levin, *Ameritopia: The Unmaking of America* (New York: threshold Editions, a Division of Simon & Schuster, Inc., 2012), pp. 23 – 36.

[30] Frederick Copleston, S.J., *A History of Philosophy: Volume I: Greece and Rome from the Pre-Socratics to Plotinus* (New York: Image Books, Doubleday, 1946), pp. 225 – 233.

[31] Mark R. Levin, *Ameritopia: The Unmaking of America* (New York: threshold Editions, a Division of Simon & Schuster, Inc., 2012), pp. 23 – 36.

[32] William J. Murray, *Utopian Road to Hell* (Washington, DC: WND Books, 2016), pp. 24 – 41.

[33] William J. Murray, *Utopian Road to Hell* (Washington, DC: WND Books, 2016), pp. 24 – 41.

[34] Thomas More, *Utopia: Translated with an Introduction and Notes by Paul Turner (Penguin Classics)* (London: Penguin Books, Copyright by Paul Turner, 1965, 2003). pp. xi – xxiv and Back Cover.

[35] Mark R. Levin, *Ameritopia: The Unmaking of America* (New York: threshold Editions, a Division of Simon & Schuster, Inc., 2012), pp. 37 – 49.

[36] Mark R. Levin, *Ameritopia: The Unmaking of America* (New York: threshold Editions, a Division of Simon & Schuster, Inc., 2012), pp. 37 – 49.

[37] Mark R. Levin, *Ameritopia: The Unmaking of America* (New York: threshold Editions, a Division of Simon & Schuster, Inc., 2012), pp. 37 – 49.

[38] Steven B. Smith, *Political Philosophy (The Open Yale Course Series)* (New Haven, CT: Yale University, 2012), pp. 140 – 164.

[39] Mark R. Levin, *Ameritopia: The Unmaking of America* (New York: threshold Editions, a Division of Simon & Schuster, Inc., 2012), p. 51 – 52.

[40] Mark R. Levin, *Ameritopia: The Unmaking of America* (New York: threshold Editions, a Division of Simon & Schuster, Inc., 2012), p. 51 – 52.

[41] Steven B. Smith, *Political Philosophy (The Open Yale Course Series)* (New Haven, CT: Yale University, 2012), pp. 140 – 164.

[42] Steven B. Smith, *Political Philosophy (The Open Yale Course Series)* (New Haven, CT: Yale University, 2012), pp. 140 – 164.

[43] Thomas Hobbes, *Leviathan: Edited with an Introduction by C. B. Macpherson Penguin Classics)* (London: Penguin Books, Copyright by C. B. Macpherson, 1968), pp. 228 – 239.

[44] Steven B. Smith, *Political Philosophy (The Open Yale Course Series)* (New Haven, CT: Yale University, 2012), pp. 140 – 164.

[45] Steven B. Smith, *Political Philosophy (The Open Yale Course Series)* (New Haven, CT: Yale University, 2012), pp. 140 – 164.

[46] Steven B. Smith, *Political Philosophy (The Open Yale Course Series)* (New Haven, CT: Yale University, 2012), pp. 140 – 164.

[47] History.com Editors, *French Revolution,* September 10, 2019, https://www.history.com/topics/france/french-revolution .

[48] History.com Editors, *French Revolution,* September 10, 2019, https://www.history.com/topics/france/french-revolution .

[49] History.com Editors, *French Revolution,* September 10, 2019, https://www.history.com/topics/france/french-revolution .

[50] Joshua Muravchik, Heaven on Earth: The Rise, Fall, and Afterlife of Socialism (New York: Encounter Books, 2002, 2003, 2019), pp. 3 – 25.

[51] Joshua Muravchik, Heaven on Earth: The Rise, Fall, and Afterlife of Socialism (New York: Encounter Books, 2002, 2003, 2019), pp. 3 – 25.

[52] Joshua Muravchik, Heaven on Earth: The Rise, Fall, and Afterlife of Socialism (New York: Encounter Books, 2002, 2003, 2019), pp. 3 – 25.

[53] Joshua Muravchik, Heaven on Earth: The Rise, Fall, and Afterlife of Socialism (New York: Encounter Books, 2002, 2003, 2019), pp. 3 – 25.

[54] Joshua Muravchik, Heaven on Earth: The Rise, Fall, and Afterlife of Socialism (New York: Encounter Books, 2002, 2003, 2019), pp. 3 – 25.

[55] Joshua Muravchik, Heaven on Earth: The Rise, Fall, and Afterlife of Socialism (New York: Encounter Books, 2002, 2003, 2019), pp. 3 – 25.

[56] Joshua Muravchik, Heaven on Earth: The Rise, Fall, and Afterlife of Socialism (New York: Encounter Books, 2002, 2003, 2019), pp. 27 – 28.

[57] Joshua Muravchik, Heaven on Earth: The Rise, Fall, and Afterlife of Socialism (New York: Encounter Books, 2002, 2003, 2019), pp. 27 – 28.

[58] Joshua Muravchik, Heaven on Earth: The Rise, Fall, and Afterlife of Socialism (New York: Encounter Books, 2002, 2003, 2019), pp. 27 – 56.

[59] Joshua Muravchik, Heaven on Earth: The Rise, Fall, and Afterlife of Socialism (New York: Encounter Books, 2002, 2003, 2019), p. 33.

[60] Robert Owen, *A New View of Society: and Other Writings* (Origami Books Pte. Ltd., 2019), p. 40.

[61] Joshua Muravchik, Heaven on Earth: The Rise, Fall, and Afterlife of Socialism (New York: Encounter Books, 2002, 2003, 2019), pp. 27 – 56.

[62] Joshua Muravchik, Heaven on Earth: The Rise, Fall, and Afterlife of Socialism (New York: Encounter Books, 2002, 2003, 2019), p. 45.

[63] Joshua Muravchik, Heaven on Earth: The Rise, Fall, and Afterlife of Socialism (New York: Encounter Books, 2002, 2003, 2019), p. 45.

[64] Joshua Muravchik, Heaven on Earth: The Rise, Fall, and Afterlife of Socialism (New York: Encounter Books, 2002, 2003, 2019), pp. 27 – 56.

[65] Note that some sources spell Friedrich Engels differently. Instead, some sources spell the name Frederik Engels.

[66] Joshua Muravchik, Heaven on Earth: The Rise, Fall, and Afterlife of Socialism (New York: Encounter Books, 2002, 2003, 2019), pp. 57 – 93.

[67] Karl Marx and Frederick Engels, *The Communist Manifesto: Introduction by Mick Hume* (London: Junius Publications Ltd. and Pluto Press, 1996, *Translation by Samuel Moore,* First

Published, 1888). Note that *The Communist Manifesto* was first published in 1848.

[68] Joshua Muravchik, Heaven on Earth: The Rise, Fall, and Afterlife of Socialism (New York: Encounter Books, 2002, 2003, 2019), pp. 57 – 93.

[69] Ludwig von Mises, *Socialism: An Economic and Sociological Analysis – Translated by J. Kahane, B.Sc. (Econ.)* (Indianapolis, IN: Liberty Fund, Inc., Bettina Bien Greaves, 1981, First English Edition Published by Jonathan Cape, 1936), p. 497.

[70] Joshua Muravchik, Heaven on Earth: The Rise, Fall, and Afterlife of Socialism (New York: Encounter Books, 2002, 2003, 2019), pp. 57 – 93.

[71] Joshua Muravchik, Heaven on Earth: The Rise, Fall, and Afterlife of Socialism (New York: Encounter Books, 2002, 2003, 2019), pp. 57 – 93.

[72] Joshua Muravchik, Heaven on Earth: The Rise, Fall, and Afterlife of Socialism (New York: Encounter Books, 2002, 2003, 2019), pp. 57 – 93.

[73] Joshua Muravchik, Heaven on Earth: The Rise, Fall, and Afterlife of Socialism (New York: Encounter Books, 2002, 2003, 2019), pp. 57 – 93.

[74] Frederick (Friedrich) Engels, *Socialism: Utopian and Scientific – With an Introduction to the French Edition by Karl Marx* (New York: Mondial, 2006).

[75] Frederick (Friedrich) Engels, *Socialism: Utopian and Scientific – With an Introduction to the French Edition by Karl Marx* (New York: Mondial, 2006).

[76] Eduard Bernstein, *Evolutionary Socialism: A Criticism and Affirmation* (Pantianos Classics, First Published in 1899), pp. iv – viii.

[77] Eduard Bernstein, *Evolutionary Socialism: A Criticism and Affirmation* (Pantianos Classics, First Published in 1899), pp. iv – viii.

[78] Ludwig von Mises, *Socialism: An Economic and Sociological Analysis – Translated by J. Kahane, B.Sc. (Econ.)* (Indianapolis,

IN: Liberty Fund, Inc., Bettina Bien Greaves, 1981, First English Edition Published by Jonathan Cape, 1936), pp. 497 – 506.

[79] Ludwig von Mises, *Socialism: An Economic and Sociological Analysis – Translated by J. Kahane, B.Sc. (Econ.)* (Indianapolis, IN: Liberty Fund, Inc., Bettina Bien Greaves, 1981, First English Edition Published by Jonathan Cape, 1936), pp. 497 – 506.

[80] Ludwig von Mises, *Socialism: An Economic and Sociological Analysis – Translated by J. Kahane, B.Sc. (Econ.)* (Indianapolis, IN: Liberty Fund, Inc., Bettina Bien Greaves, 1981, First English Edition Published by Jonathan Cape, 1936), pp. 497 – 506.

[81] Ludwig von Mises, *Socialism: An Economic and Sociological Analysis – Translated by J. Kahane, B.Sc. (Econ.)* (Indianapolis, IN: Liberty Fund, Inc., Bettina Bien Greaves, 1981, First English Edition Published by Jonathan Cape, 1936), pp. 497 – 506.

[82] Ludwig von Mises, *Socialism: An Economic and Sociological Analysis – Translated by J. Kahane, B.Sc. (Econ.)* (Indianapolis, IN: Liberty Fund, Inc., Bettina Bien Greaves, 1981, First English Edition Published by Jonathan Cape, 1936), pp. 497 – 506.

[83] Ludwig von Mises, *Socialism: An Economic and Sociological Analysis – Translated by J. Kahane, B.Sc. (Econ.)* (Indianapolis, IN: Liberty Fund, Inc., Bettina Bien Greaves, 1981, First English Edition Published by Jonathan Cape, 1936), pp. 497 – 506.

[84] Joshua Muravchik, Heaven on Earth: The Rise, Fall, and Afterlife of Socialism (New York: Encounter Books, 2002, 2003, 2019), pp. 395 – 398.

[85] Joshua Muravchik, Heaven on Earth: The Rise, Fall, and Afterlife of Socialism (New York: Encounter Books, 2002, 2003, 2019), pp. 395 – 398.

[86] Richard Pipes, *A Concise History of the Russian Revolution* (New York: Vintage Books, A Division of Random House, Inc., 1995), pp. 113 – 149.

[87] Richard Pipes, *A Concise History of the Russian Revolution* (New York: Vintage Books, A Division of Random House, Inc., 1995), pp. 113 – 149.

[88] Richard Pipes, *A Concise History of the Russian Revolution* (New York: Vintage Books, A Division of Random House, Inc., 1995), pp. 382 – 386.

[89] Richard Pipes, *A Concise History of the Russian Revolution* (New York: Vintage Books, A Division of Random House, Inc., 1995), pp. 113 – 149.

[90] Richard Pipes, *A Concise History of the Russian Revolution* (New York: Vintage Books, A Division of Random House, Inc., 1995), pp. 113 – 149.

[91] Richard Pipes, *A Concise History of the Russian Revolution* (New York: Vintage Books, A Division of Random House, Inc., 1995), pp. 113 – 149, 392 – 394.

[92] Richard Pipes, *A Concise History of the Russian Revolution* (New York: Vintage Books, A Division of Random House, Inc., 1995), p. 105.

[93] Richard Pipes, *A Concise History of the Russian Revolution* (New York: Vintage Books, A Division of Random House, Inc., 1995), p. 118.

[94] Richard Pipes, *A Concise History of the Russian Revolution* (New York: Vintage Books, A Division of Random House, Inc., 1995), pp. 101 – 104.

[95] Richard Pipes, *A Concise History of the Russian Revolution* (New York: Vintage Books, A Division of Random House, Inc., 1995), pp. 404 – 405.

[96] Richard Pipes, *A Concise History of the Russian Revolution* (New York: Vintage Books, A Division of Random House, Inc., 1995), pp. 404 – 405.

[97] Joshua Muravchik, Heaven on Earth: The Rise, Fall, and Afterlife of Socialism (New York: Encounter Books, 2002, 2003, 2019), pp. 128 – 129.

[98] Joshua Muravchik, Heaven on Earth: The Rise, Fall, and Afterlife of Socialism (New York: Encounter Books, 2002, 2003, 2019), pp. 140 – 142.

[99] Joshua Muravchik, Heaven on Earth: The Rise, Fall, and Afterlife of Socialism (New York: Encounter Books, 2002, 2003, 2019), p. 145.

[100] Stephane Courtois, et. al., *The Black Book of Communism: Crimes, Terror, Repression, Translated by Jonathan Murphy and Mark Kramer, Consulting Editor Mark Kramer* (Cambridge, MA: Harvard University Press, Copyright © 1999 by the President and Fellows of Harvard College), pp. 1 – 31.

[101] Stephane Courtois, et. al., *The Black Book of Communism: Crimes, Terror, Repression, Translated by Jonathan Murphy and Mark Kramer, Consulting Editor Mark Kramer* (Cambridge, MA: Harvard University Press, Copyright © 1999 by the President and Fellows of Harvard College), pp. 33 – 268.

[102] Richard Pipes, *A Concise History of the Russian Revolution* (New York: Vintage Books, A Division of Random House, Inc., 1995), pp. 404 – 405.

[103] Thomas J. DiLorenzo, *The Problem with Socialism* (Washington, DC: Regnery Publishing, 2016), pp. 65 – 76.

[104] Thomas J. DiLorenzo, *The Problem with Socialism* (Washington, DC: Regnery Publishing, 2016), pp. 65 – 76.

[105] Jonah Goldberg, *Liberal Fascism: The Secret History of the American Left from Mussolini to the Politics of Meaning* (New York: Doubleday, 2007), pp. 70 – 71.

[106] Jonah Goldberg, *Liberal Fascism: The Secret History of the American Left from Mussolini to the Politics of Meaning* (New York: Doubleday, 2007), pp. 71 – 72.

[107] Thomas J. DiLorenzo, *The Problem with Socialism* (Washington, DC: Regnery Publishing, 2016), pp. 65 – 76.

[108] Thomas J. DiLorenzo, *The Problem with Socialism* (Washington, DC: Regnery Publishing, 2016), pp. 65 – 76.

[109] Thomas J. DiLorenzo, *The Problem with Socialism* (Washington, DC: Regnery Publishing, 2016), pp. 65 – 76.

[110] Joshua Muravchik, Heaven on Earth: The Rise, Fall, and Afterlife of Socialism (New York: Encounter Books, 2002, 2003, 2019), pp. 167 – 168.

[111] Joshua Muravchik, Heaven on Earth: The Rise, Fall, and Afterlife of Socialism (New York: Encounter Books, 2002, 2003, 2019), pp. 167 – 168.

[112] Thomas J. DiLorenzo, *The Problem with Socialism* (Washington, DC: Regnery Publishing, 2016), pp. 65 – 76.

[113] R. J. Rummel, *Death by Government* (New York: Routledge, Routledge is an imprint of Taylor & Francis Group, First published 1994 by Transaction Publishers, Taylor & Francis, 1994), pp. 111 – 122.

[114] R. J. Rummel, *Death by Government* (New York: Routledge, Routledge is an imprint of Taylor & Francis Group, First published 1994 by Transaction Publishers, Taylor & Francis, 1994), pp. 111 – 122.

[115] Thomas J. DiLorenzo, *The Problem with Socialism* (Washington, DC: Regnery Publishing, 2016), pp. 65 – 76.

[116] Joshua Muravchik, Heaven on Earth: The Rise, Fall, and Afterlife of Socialism (New York: Encounter Books, 2002, 2003, 2019), pp. 143 – 175.

[117] Joshua Muravchik, Heaven on Earth: The Rise, Fall, and Afterlife of Socialism (New York: Encounter Books, 2002, 2003, 2019), pp. 161 – 173.

[118] Joshua Muravchik, Heaven on Earth: The Rise, Fall, and Afterlife of Socialism (New York: Encounter Books, 2002, 2003, 2019), pp. 143 – 175.

[119] Jonah Goldberg, *Liberal Fascism: The Secret History of the American Left from Mussolini to the Politics of Meaning* (New York: Doubleday, 2007), pp. 31 – 33.

[120] Jonah Goldberg, *Liberal Fascism: The Secret History of the American Left from Mussolini to the Politics of Meaning* (New York: Doubleday, 2007), pp. 31 – 33.

[121] Thomas J. DiLorenzo, *The Problem with Socialism* (Washington, DC: Regnery Publishing, 2016), pp. 70 – 71.

[122] Joshua Muravchik, Heaven on Earth: The Rise, Fall, and Afterlife of Socialism (New York: Encounter Books, 2002, 2003, 2019), pp. 335 – 366.

[123] "The Kibbutz and Moshav: History and Overview," *Jewish Virtual Library: A Project of AICE* (Chevy Chase, MD: American-Israeli Cooperative Enterprise, 1998 – 2019), https://www.jewishvirtuallibrary.org/history-and-overview-of-the-kibbutz-movement .

[124] Joshua Muravchik, Heaven on Earth: The Rise, Fall, and Afterlife of Socialism (New York: Encounter Books, 2002, 2003, 2019), p. 336.

[125] Joshua Muravchik, Heaven on Earth: The Rise, Fall, and Afterlife of Socialism (New York: Encounter Books, 2002, 2003, 2019), pp. 335 – 366.

[126] Joshua Muravchik, Heaven on Earth: The Rise, Fall, and Afterlife of Socialism (New York: Encounter Books, 2002, 2003, 2019), p. 335.

[127] Joshua Muravchik, Heaven on Earth: The Rise, Fall, and Afterlife of Socialism (New York: Encounter Books, 2002, 2003, 2019), pp. 335 – 366.

[128] Joshua Muravchik, Heaven on Earth: The Rise, Fall, and Afterlife of Socialism (New York: Encounter Books, 2002, 2003, 2019), pp. 335 – 366.

[129] Joshua Muravchik, Heaven on Earth: The Rise, Fall, and Afterlife of Socialism (New York: Encounter Books, 2002, 2003, 2019), pp. 335 – 366.

[130] Joshua Muravchik, Heaven on Earth: The Rise, Fall, and Afterlife of Socialism (New York: Encounter Books, 2002, 2003, 2019), p. 348.

[131] R. J. Rummel, *Death by Government* (New York: Routledge, Routledge is an imprint of Taylor & Francis Group, First published 1994 by Transaction Publishers, Taylor & Francis, 1994), pp. 91 – 109.

[132] R. J. Rummel, *Death by Government* (New York: Routledge, Routledge is an imprint of Taylor & Francis Group, First published 1994 by Transaction Publishers, Taylor & Francis, 1994), pp. 91 – 109.

[133] R. J. Rummel, *Death by Government* (New York: Routledge, Routledge is an imprint of Taylor & Francis Group, First published 1994 by Transaction Publishers, Taylor & Francis, 1994), pp. 91 – 109.

[134] R. J. Rummel, *Death by Government* (New York: Routledge, Routledge is an imprint of Taylor & Francis Group, First published 1994 by Transaction Publishers, Taylor & Francis, 1994), pp. 91 – 109.

[135] R. J. Rummel, *Death by Government* (New York: Routledge, Routledge is an imprint of Taylor & Francis Group, First published 1994 by Transaction Publishers, Taylor & Francis, 1994), pp. 91 – 109.

[136] Stephane Courtois, et. al., *The Black Book of Communism: Crimes, Terror, Repression, Translated by Jonathan Murphy and Mark Kramer, Consulting Editor Mark Kramer* (Cambridge, MA: Harvard University Press, Copyright © 1999 by the President and Fellows of Harvard College), pp. 1 – 31.

[137] Joshua Muravchik, Heaven on Earth: The Rise, Fall, and Afterlife of Socialism (New York: Encounter Books, 2002, 2003, 2019), pp. 273 – 312.

[138] Joshua Muravchik, Heaven on Earth: The Rise, Fall, and Afterlife of Socialism (New York: Encounter Books, 2002, 2003, 2019), pp. 273 – 312.

[139] Joshua Muravchik, Heaven on Earth: The Rise, Fall, and Afterlife of Socialism (New York: Encounter Books, 2002, 2003, 2019), pp. 273 – 312.

[140] Joshua Muravchik, Heaven on Earth: The Rise, Fall, and Afterlife of Socialism (New York: Encounter Books, 2002, 2003, 2019), pp. 273 – 312.

[141] Joshua Muravchik, Heaven on Earth: The Rise, Fall, and Afterlife of Socialism (New York: Encounter Books, 2002, 2003, 2019), pp. 177 – 203 and pp. 313 – 333.

[142] Joshua Muravchik, Heaven on Earth: The Rise, Fall, and Afterlife of Socialism (New York: Encounter Books, 2002, 2003, 2019), pp. 177 – 203.

[143] Joshua Muravchik, Heaven on Earth: The Rise, Fall, and Afterlife of Socialism (New York: Encounter Books, 2002, 2003, 2019), pp. 177 – 203.

[144] Joshua Muravchik, Heaven on Earth: The Rise, Fall, and Afterlife of Socialism (New York: Encounter Books, 2002, 2003, 2019), pp. 177 – 203.

[145] Joshua Muravchik, Heaven on Earth: The Rise, Fall, and Afterlife of Socialism (New York: Encounter Books, 2002, 2003, 2019), pp. 186 – 187.

[146] John Bew, *Clement Attlee: The Man Who Made Modern Britain* (New York: Oxford University Press, 2017), pp. 247 – 253.

[147] Joshua Muravchik, Heaven on Earth: The Rise, Fall, and Afterlife of Socialism (New York: Encounter Books, 2002, 2003, 2019), pp. 177 – 203.

[148] Joshua Muravchik, Heaven on Earth: The Rise, Fall, and Afterlife of Socialism (New York: Encounter Books, 2002, 2003, 2019), pp. 177 – 203.

[149] Joshua Muravchik, Heaven on Earth: The Rise, Fall, and Afterlife of Socialism (New York: Encounter Books, 2002, 2003, 2019), pp. 177 – 203.

[150] John Bew, *Clement Attlee: The Man Who Made Modern Britain* (New York: Oxford University Press, 2017), p. 391.

[151] John Bew, *Clement Attlee: The Man Who Made Modern Britain* (New York: Oxford University Press, 2017), p. 391.

[152] Joshua Muravchik, Heaven on Earth: The Rise, Fall, and Afterlife of Socialism (New York: Encounter Books, 2002, 2003, 2019), pp. 177 – 203.

[153] Joshua Muravchik, Heaven on Earth: The Rise, Fall, and Afterlife of Socialism (New York: Encounter Books, 2002, 2003, 2019), pp. 177 – 203.

[154] Joshua Muravchik, Heaven on Earth: The Rise, Fall, and Afterlife of Socialism (New York: Encounter Books, 2002, 2003, 2019), pp. 177 – 203, pp. 313 – 333.

[155] Joshua Muravchik, Heaven on Earth: The Rise, Fall, and Afterlife of Socialism (New York: Encounter Books, 2002, 2003, 2019), pp. 313 – 333.

[156] Joshua Muravchik, Heaven on Earth: The Rise, Fall, and Afterlife of Socialism (New York: Encounter Books, 2002, 2003, 2019), pp. 313 – 333.

[157] Joshua Muravchik, Heaven on Earth: The Rise, Fall, and Afterlife of Socialism (New York: Encounter Books, 2002, 2003, 2019), pp. 313 – 333.

[158] Gerard Francis Lameiro, *America's Economic War – Your Freedom, Money and Life: A Citizen's Handbook for Understanding the War between American Capitalism and Socialism* (Fort Collins, CO: Gerard Francis Lameiro, Ph.D., 2009), pp. 114 – 119.

[159] Joshua Muravchik, Heaven on Earth: The Rise, Fall, and Afterlife of Socialism (New York: Encounter Books, 2002, 2003, 2019), pp. 313 – 333.

[160] Tony Blair, *A Journey: My Political Life* (New York: Vintage Books, A Division of Random House Inc., 2011), pp. 78 – 85.

[161] Oscar Wilde, *Goodreads,* (Goodreads: Copyright, 2019), https://www.goodreads.com/quotes/558084-imitation-is-the-sincerest-form-of-flattery-that-mediocrity-can .

[162] Liam Halligan, "How did Tony Blair leave the British economy?" *The Telegraph,* https://www.telegraph.co.uk/finance/economics/10992792/How-did-Tony-Blair-leave-the-British-economy.html, July 26, 2014.

[163] Liam Halligan, "How did Tony Blair leave the British economy?" *The Telegraph,* https://www.telegraph.co.uk/finance/economics/10992792/How-did-Tony-Blair-leave-the-British-economy.html, July 26, 2014.

[164] Joshua Muravchik, Heaven on Earth: The Rise, Fall, and Afterlife of Socialism (New York: Encounter Books, 2002, 2003, 2019), pp. 237 – 271.

[165] Joshua Muravchik, Heaven on Earth: The Rise, Fall, and Afterlife of Socialism (New York: Encounter Books, 2002, 2003, 2019), pp. 237 – 271.

[166] Joshua Muravchik, Heaven on Earth: The Rise, Fall, and Afterlife of Socialism (New York: Encounter Books, 2002, 2003, 2019), pp. 237 – 271.

[167] Joshua Muravchik, Heaven on Earth: The Rise, Fall, and Afterlife of Socialism (New York: Encounter Books, 2002, 2003, 2019), pp. 237 – 271.

[168] Joshua Muravchik, Heaven on Earth: The Rise, Fall, and Afterlife of Socialism (New York: Encounter Books, 2002, 2003, 2019), p. 252.

[169] Joshua Muravchik, Heaven on Earth: The Rise, Fall, and Afterlife of Socialism (New York: Encounter Books, 2002, 2003, 2019), pp. 266 – 268.

[170] Michael Watson, "When the Labor Unions Fought Socialism," Capital Research Center, April 3, 2019, https://capitalresearch.org/article/when-the-labor-unions-fought-socialism/ .

[171] Michael Watson, "When the Labor Unions Fought Socialism," Capital Research Center, April 3, 2019, https://capitalresearch.org/article/when-the-labor-unions-fought-socialism/ .

[172] Justin Haskins, "America's Public Schools Have Become Socialist Indoctrination Factories," Townhall.com/Salem Media, January 28, 2019, https://townhall.com/columnists/justinhaskins/2019/01/28/americas-public-schools-have-become-socialist-indoctrination-factories-n2540323 .

[173] Justin Haskins, "America's Public Schools Have Become Socialist Indoctrination Factories," Townhall.com/Salem Media, January 28, 2019, https://townhall.com/columnists/justinhaskins/2019/01/28/americas-public-schools-have-become-socialist-indoctrination-factories-n2540323 .

[174] Justin Haskins, "America's Public Schools Have Become Socialist Indoctrination Factories," Townhall.com/Salem Media, January 28, 2019, https://townhall.com/columnists/justinhaskins/2019/01/28/americas-public-schools-have-become-socialist-indoctrination-factories-n2540323 .

[175] Justin Haskins, "America's Public Schools Have Become Socialist Indoctrination Factories," Townhall.com/Salem Media, January 28, 2019, https://townhall.com/columnists/justinhaskins/2019/01/28/americas-public-schools-have-become-socialist-indoctrination-factories-n2540323 .

[176] Investor's Business Daily Editorial, "Media Bias: Pretty Much All Of Journalism Now Leans Left, Study Shows," *Investor's Business Daily,* November 16, 2018, https://www.investors.com/politics/editorials/media-bias-left-study/ .

[177] Investor's Business Daily Editorial, "Media Bias: Pretty Much All Of Journalism Now Leans Left, Study Shows," *Investor's Business Daily,* November 16, 2018, https://www.investors.com/politics/editorials/media-bias-left-study/ .

[178] Carrie Sheffield, "Pew Study Reveals Why Media Has Anti-'Flyover State' Bias," Accuracy in Media, October 29, 2019, https://www.aim.org/aim-investigates/pew-study-reveals-why-media-has-anti-flyover-state-bias/ .

[179] Carrie Sheffield, "Pew Study Reveals Why Media Has Anti-'Flyover State' Bias," Accuracy in Media, October 29, 2019, https://www.aim.org/aim-investigates/pew-study-reveals-why-media-has-anti-flyover-state-bias/ .

[180] Nicholas Fondacaro, "ABC, NBC Excited to Learn 'Centrist' Bloomberg Might Run in 2020," MRC NewsBusters, November 7, 2019, https://www.newsbusters.org/blogs/nb/nicholas-fondacaro/2019/11/07/abc-nbc-excited-learn-centrist-bloomberg-might-run-2020 .

181 Nicholas Fondacaro, "New NBC Series Only Looks at 'What Matters' to Democratic Voters," MRC NewsBusters, November 5, 2019, https://www.newsbusters.org/blogs/nb/nicholas-fondacaro/2019/11/05/new-nbc-series-only-looks-what-matters-democratic-voters .

182 Emma Tobin and Ivana Kottasová, "11,000 scientists warn of 'untold suffering' caused by climate change," CNN, November 6, 2019, https://www.cnn.com/2019/11/05/world/climate-emergency-scientists-warning-intl-trnd/index.html .

183 Denise Chow, "More than 11,000 scientists issue fresh warning: Earth faces a climate emergency," NBC News, November 5, 2019, https://www.nbcnews.com/science/environment/more-11-000-scientists-issue-fresh-warning-earth-faces-climate-n1076851 .

184 John Hinderaker, "11,000 SCIENTISTS? JUST KIDDING," Power Line, November 8, 2019, https://www.powerlineblog.com/archives/2019/11/11000-scientists-just-kidding.php .

185 Ashley Rae Goldenberg and Dan Gainor, "CENSORED! How Online Media Companies Are Suppressing Conservative Speech," MRC NewsBusters, April 16, 2018, https://www.newsbusters.org/blogs/culture/ashley-rae-goldenberg/2018/04/16/censored-how-online-media-companies-are-suppressing .

186 Ashley Rae Goldenberg and Dan Gainor, "CENSORED! How Online Media Companies Are Suppressing Conservative Speech," MRC NewsBusters, April 16, 2018, https://www.newsbusters.org/blogs/culture/ashley-rae-goldenberg/2018/04/16/censored-how-online-media-companies-are-suppressing .

187 Ashley Rae Goldenberg and Dan Gainor, "CENSORED! How Online Media Companies Are Suppressing Conservative

Speech," MRC NewsBusters, April 16, 2018, https://www.newsbusters.org/blogs/culture/ashley-rae-goldenberg/2018/04/16/censored-how-online-media-companies-are-suppressing .

[188] Ashley Rae Goldenberg and Dan Gainor, "CENSORED! How Online Media Companies Are Suppressing Conservative Speech," MRC NewsBusters, April 16, 2018, https://www.newsbusters.org/blogs/culture/ashley-rae-goldenberg/2018/04/16/censored-how-online-media-companies-are-suppressing .

[189] Ashley Rae Goldenberg and Dan Gainor, "CENSORED! How Online Media Companies Are Suppressing Conservative Speech," MRC NewsBusters, April 16, 2018, https://www.newsbusters.org/blogs/culture/ashley-rae-goldenberg/2018/04/16/censored-how-online-media-companies-are-suppressing .

[190] Sean Captain, "Meet the Silicon Valley socialists who are pushing a tech worker uprising," *Fast Company,* July 17, 2018, https://www.fastcompany.com/90202378/meet-the-silicon-valley-socialists-pushing-a-surge-in-tech-worker-activism .

[191] Sean Captain, "Meet the Silicon Valley socialists who are pushing a tech worker uprising," *Fast Company,* July 17, 2018, https://www.fastcompany.com/90202378/meet-the-silicon-valley-socialists-pushing-a-surge-in-tech-worker-activism .

[192] Nicholas Clairmont, ""Those Who Do Not Learn History Are Doomed To Repeat It." Really?" Big Think, July 31, 2013, https://bigthink.com/the-proverbial-skeptic/those-who-do-not-learn-history-doomed-to-repeat-it-really .

[193] Sean Captain, "Meet the Silicon Valley socialists who are pushing a tech worker uprising," *Fast Company,* July 17, 2018, https://www.fastcompany.com/90202378/meet-the-silicon-valley-socialists-pushing-a-surge-in-tech-worker-activism .

[194] "DTN – Guides: SUMMARY: ARTS AND CULTURE," DiscoverTheNetworks.org, Copyright 2003 – 2015 DiscoverTheNetworks.org,

http://archive.discoverthenetworks.org/guideDesc.asp?type=art .

[195] "HOLLYWOOD AND COMMUNISM/SOCIALISM," DiscoverTheNetworks.org, Copyright 2003 – 2015 DiscoverTheNetworks.org, http://archive.discoverthenetworks.org/guideDesc.asp?type=art .

[196] "HOLLYWOOD AND COMMUNISM/SOCIALISM," DiscoverTheNetworks.org, Copyright 2003 – 2015 DiscoverTheNetworks.org, http://archive.discoverthenetworks.org/guideDesc.asp?type=art .

[197] "HOLLYWOOD AND COMMUNISM/SOCIALISM," DiscoverTheNetworks.org, Copyright 2003 – 2015 DiscoverTheNetworks.org, http://archive.discoverthenetworks.org/guideDesc.asp?type=art .

[198] Jonathan Leaf, "Radical Socialists in Hollywood Keep Falsifying History and Whitewashing Communists," The Stream, July 23, 2016, https://stream.org/radical-socialists-hollywood-keep-falsifying-history-whitewashing-communists/ .

[199] "HOLLYWOOD AND COMMUNISM/SOCIALISM," DiscoverTheNetworks.org, Copyright 2003 – 2015 DiscoverTheNetworks.org, http://archive.discoverthenetworks.org/guideDesc.asp?type=art .

[200] "LEFTWING BIAS IN THE ENTERTAINMENT INDUSTRY," DiscoverTheNetworks.org, Copyright 2003 – 2015 DiscoverTheNetworks.org, http://archive.discoverthenetworks.org/guideDesc.asp?type=art .

[201] Marina Villeneuva, "Maine becomes 8th state to legalize assisted suicide," The Associated Press, June 12, 2019,

Copyright by The Associated Press, 2019,
https://apnews.com/7f0fe9d789294a02852c1669c892f382 .

[202] Gerard Francis Lameiro, *Renewing America and Its Heritage of Freedom: What Freedom-Loving Americans Can Do to Help* (Fort Collins, CO: Gerard Francis Lameiro, 2014), pp. 29 – 35.

[203] Gerard Francis Lameiro, *Renewing America and Its Heritage of Freedom: What Freedom-Loving Americans Can Do to Help* (Fort Collins, CO: Gerard Francis Lameiro, 2014), pp. 123 – 142.

[204] The Week Staff, "How marriage has changed over centuries," The Week, June 1, 2012, Copyright by The Week Publications Inc., 2019,
https://theweek.com/articles/475141/how-marriage-changed-over-centuries .

[205] Frederick Engels, *The Origin of the Family: Private Property and the State,* Translated by Ernest Untermann (Honolulu, HI: University Press on the Pacific, 2001, Reprinted from the 1902 Edition), p. 79.

[206] Gabriele Kuby, *The Global Sexual Revolution: Destruction of Freedom in the Name of Freedom,* Translated by James Patrick Kirchner (Kettering, OH: LifeSite, an Imprint of Angelico Press, 2015), p. 22.

[207] Gabriele Kuby, *The Global Sexual Revolution: Destruction of Freedom in the Name of Freedom,* Translated by James Patrick Kirchner (Kettering, OH: LifeSite, an Imprint of Angelico Press, 2015), pp. 3 – 11.

[208] John R. Lott, Jr., *More Guns, Less Crime: Understanding Crime and Gun Control Laws, Third Edition* (Chicago, IL: The University of Chicago Press, The University of Chicago, 1998, 2000, 2010), p. 20.

[209] John R. Lott, Jr., *More Guns, Less Crime: Understanding Crime and Gun Control Laws, Third Edition* (Chicago, IL: The University of Chicago Press, The University of Chicago, 1998, 2000, 2010), p. 21.

210 John R. Lott, Jr., *More Guns, Less Crime: Understanding Crime and Gun Control Laws, Third Edition* (Chicago, IL: The University of Chicago Press, The University of Chicago, 1998, 2000, 2010), p. 21.

211 Adam Mill, "Does Gun Control Reduce Murder? Let's Run The Numbers Across the World," The Federalist, April 3, 2018, https://thefederalist.com/2018/04/03/gun-control-reduce-murder-lets-run-numbers-across-world/ .

212 Adam Mill, "Does Gun Control Reduce Murder? Let's Run The Numbers Across the World," The Federalist, April 3, 2018, https://thefederalist.com/2018/04/03/gun-control-reduce-murder-lets-run-numbers-across-world/ .

213 Stephen P. Halbrook, *Gun Control in the Third Reich: Disarming the Jews and the "Enemies of the State"'* (Oakland, CA: The Independent Institute, 2013).

214 U. S. Geological Survey, "How many counties are there in the United States?" U.S. Geological Survey, U.S. Department of the Interior, No Publication Date Found on Website, https://www.usgs.gov/faqs/how-many-counties-are-there-united-states .

215 Gerard Lameiro, *More Great News for America: The Dawning of the New Conservative Era (How and Why the Good Guys Win in the End!)* (Fort Collins, CO: Gerard Francis Lameiro, Ph.D., 2018), p. 38.

216 Gerard Lameiro, *More Great News for America: The Dawning of the New Conservative Era (How and Why the Good Guys Win in the End!)* (Fort Collins, CO: Gerard Francis Lameiro, Ph.D., 2018), p. 38.

217 "Agreement Among the States to Elect the President by National Popular Vote," National Popular Vote, No Publication Date Found on Website, https://www.nationalpopularvote.com/written-explanation .

218 Emily Davies, "Colorado approved a national popular vote law. Now it might be repealed." *The Washington Post,* August 2, 2019, https://www.washingtonpost.com/politics/colorado-

approved-a-national-popular-vote-law-now-it-might-be-repealed/2019/08/02/a305b1de-b468-11e9-8e94-71a35969e4d8_story.html .

219 "Heritage Explains: Voter Fraud," *The Heritage Foundation,* No Publication Date Found on Website, https://www.heritage.org/election-integrity/heritage-explains/voter-fraud .

220 John Fund and Hans A. von Spakovsky, "Voter Fraud Exists – Even Though Many in the Media Claim It Doesn't," *The Heritage Foundation,* October 29, 2018, https://www.heritage.org/election-integrity/commentary/voter-fraud-exists-even-though-many-the-media-claim-it-doesnt .

221 John Fund and Hans A. von Spakovsky, "Voter Fraud Exists – Even Though Many in the Media Claim It Doesn't," *The Heritage Foundation,* October 29, 2018, https://www.heritage.org/election-integrity/commentary/voter-fraud-exists-even-though-many-the-media-claim-it-doesnt .

222 Hans A. von Spakovsky, "Vote Harvesting A Recipe for Coercion and Election Fraud," *The Heritage Foundation,* October 30, 2019, https://www.heritage.org/election-integrity/commentary/vote-harvesting-recipe-coercion-and-election-fraud .

223 Hans A. von Spakovsky, "Vote Harvesting A Recipe for Coercion and Election Fraud," *The Heritage Foundation,* October 30, 2019, https://www.heritage.org/election-integrity/commentary/vote-harvesting-recipe-coercion-and-election-fraud .

224 Hans A. von Spakovsky, "Vote Harvesting A Recipe for Coercion and Election Fraud," *The Heritage Foundation,* October 30, 2019, https://www.heritage.org/election-integrity/commentary/vote-harvesting-recipe-coercion-and-election-fraud .

[225] Hans A. von Spakovsky, "Crimes by Illegal Immigrants Widespread Across U. S. – Sanctuaries Shouldn't Shield Them," *The Heritage Foundation,* September 3, 2019, https://www.heritage.org/crime-and-justice/commentary/crimes-illegal-immigrants-widespread-across-us-sanctuaries-shouldnt .

[226] Hans A. von Spakovsky, "Crimes by Illegal Immigrants Widespread Across U. S. – Sanctuaries Shouldn't Shield Them," *The Heritage Foundation,* September 3, 2019, https://www.heritage.org/crime-and-justice/commentary/crimes-illegal-immigrants-widespread-across-us-sanctuaries-shouldnt .

[227] Immigration Reform Law Institute (IRLI) Staff, "New FAIR Study: Illegal Immigration Costs $116 billion Annually," Immigration Reform Law Institute, September 27, 2017, https://www.irli.org/single-post/2017/09/27/New-FAIR-Study-Illegal-Immigration-Costs-116-billion-Annually?gclid=CjwKCAiAws7uBRAkEiwAMIbZjsEJFBvvHHvKUR1bS21V7ovv9dFJvAWWygiwG9CsSq3YQ3uc17SWABoCcXAQAvD_BwE .

[228] Daniella Genovese, "Trump: Illegal immigration costs US over $300B a year," Fox Business, September 13, 2019, https://www.foxbusiness.com/economy/trump-illegal-immigration-costs-the-us-over-300b-a-year .

[229] See the voter fraud example dated 2014 in: "Heritage Explains: Voter Fraud," *The Heritage Foundation,* No Publication Date Found on Website, https://www.heritage.org/election-integrity/heritage-explains/voter-fraud .

[230] Gerard Francis Lameiro, *Renewing America and Its Heritage of Freedom: What Freedom-Loving Americans Can Do to Help* (Fort Collins, CO: Gerard Francis Lameiro, 2014).

[231] Some of the material in this section was adapted from my 2010 book: Gerard Francis Lameiro, *America's Economic War – Your Freedom, Money and Life: A Citizen's Handbook for*

Understanding the War between American Capitalism and Socialism (Fort Collins, CO: Gerard Francis Lameiro, Ph.D., 2009), pp. 146 – 150.

[232] Ludwig von Mises, *Human Action: A Treatise on Economics, Third Revised Edition* (Chicago, IL: Contemporary Books, Inc., 1966), p. 851.

[233] Arthur C. Brooks, "What Really Buys Happiness: Not income equality, but mobility and opportunity," *City Journal,* Summer 2007, https://www.city-journal.org/html/what-really-buys-happiness-13028.html .

[234] Arthur C. Brooks, "What Really Buys Happiness: Not income equality, but mobility and opportunity," *City Journal,* Summer 2007, https://www.city-journal.org/html/what-really-buys-happiness-13028.html .

[235] Arthur C. Brooks, "What Really Buys Happiness: Not income equality, but mobility and opportunity," *City Journal,* Summer 2007, https://www.city-journal.org/html/what-really-buys-happiness-13028.html .

[236] Joseph A. Schumpeter, *Capitalism, Socialism and Democracy* (New York, NY: Harper & Row publishers, Inc., 1975), pp. 82 -83.

[237] Ludwig von Mises, *Socialism: An Economic and Sociological Analysis – Translated by J. Kahane, B.Sc. (Econ.)* (Indianapolis, IN: Liberty Fund, Inc., Bettina Bien Greaves, 1981, First English Edition Published by Jonathan Cape, 1936), p. 306.

[238] Ludwig von Mises, *Socialism: An Economic and Sociological Analysis – Translated by J. Kahane, B.Sc. (Econ.)* (Indianapolis, IN: Liberty Fund, Inc., Bettina Bien Greaves, 1981, First English Edition Published by Jonathan Cape, 1936), p. 306.

[239] Ludwig von Mises, *Socialism: An Economic and Sociological Analysis – Translated by J. Kahane, B.Sc. (Econ.)* (Indianapolis, IN: Liberty Fund, Inc., Bettina Bien Greaves, 1981, First English Edition Published by Jonathan Cape, 1936), p. 306.

[240] Nicole Kaeding, "Taxable Income vs. Book Income: Why Some Corporations Pay No Income Tax," Tax Foundation, May

2, 2019, Copyright Tax Foundation 2019,
https://taxfoundation.org/why-corporations-pay-no-income-tax/ .

[241] Reviewed by Alicia Tuovila, "Generally Accepted Accounting Principles (GAAP)," Investopedia, October 11, 2019, https://www.investopedia.com/terms/g/gaap.asp .

[242] Nicole Kaeding, "Taxable Income vs. Book Income: Why Some Corporations Pay No Income Tax," Tax Foundation, May 2, 2019, Copyright Tax Foundation 2019,
https://taxfoundation.org/why-corporations-pay-no-income-tax/ .

[243] Nicole Kaeding, "Taxable Income vs. Book Income: Why Some Corporations Pay No Income Tax," Tax Foundation, May 2, 2019, Copyright Tax Foundation 2019,
https://taxfoundation.org/why-corporations-pay-no-income-tax/ .

[244] Nicole Kaeding, "Taxable Income vs. Book Income: Why Some Corporations Pay No Income Tax," Tax Foundation, May 2, 2019, Copyright Tax Foundation 2019,
https://taxfoundation.org/why-corporations-pay-no-income-tax/ .

[245] Gerard Francis Lameiro, GreatNewsForAmerica.com, Copyright by Gerard Francis Lameiro, Ph.D. 2009 – 2018. https://greatnewsforamerica.com/quotes/ .

[246] Some of the material in this section was adapted from my 2010 book: Gerard Francis Lameiro, *America's Economic War – Your Freedom, Money and Life: A Citizen's Handbook for Understanding the War between American Capitalism and Socialism* (Fort Collins, CO: Gerard Francis Lameiro, Ph.D., 2009), pp. 144 – 146.

[247] Heritage Explains, "How to Fight the War on Poverty," *The Heritage Foundation,* Copyright by The Heritage Foundation 2019, https://www.heritage.org/poverty-and-inequality/heritage-explains/how-fight-the-war-poverty .

[248] Heritage Explains, "How to Fight the War on Poverty," *The Heritage Foundation,* Copyright by The Heritage Foundation 2019, https://www.heritage.org/poverty-and-inequality/heritage-explains/how-fight-the-war-poverty .

[249] Heritage Explains, "How to Fight the War on Poverty," *The Heritage Foundation,* Copyright by The Heritage Foundation 2019, https://www.heritage.org/poverty-and-inequality/heritage-explains/how-fight-the-war-poverty .

[250] Charles C. W. Cooke, "Socialism Is Not Democratic," *National Review,* May 16, 2019, Copyright by National Review 2019, https://www.nationalreview.com/magazine/2019/06/03/socialism-is-not-democratic/ .

[251] Gerard Francis Lameiro, *Renewing America and Its Heritage of Freedom: What Freedom-Loving Americans Can Do to Help* (Fort Collins, CO: Gerard Francis Lameiro, 2014).

[252] Charles C. W. Cooke, "Socialism Is Not Democratic," *National Review,* May 16, 2019, Copyright by National Review 2019, https://www.nationalreview.com/magazine/2019/06/03/socialism-is-not-democratic/ .

[253] Karl Marx and Frederick Engels, *The Communist Manifesto: Introduction by Mick Hume* (London: Junius Publications Ltd. and Pluto Press, 1996, *Translation by Samuel Moore,* First Published, 1888). Note that *The Communist Manifesto* was first published in 1848. The quote is taken from p. 17.

[254] Donald Billings and E. Barry Asmus, "The Morality of Capitalism," Foundation for Economic Education, September 1, 1985, https://fee.org/articles/the-morality-of-capitalism/ .

[255] Donald Billings and E. Barry Asmus, "The Morality of Capitalism," Foundation for Economic Education, September 1, 1985, https://fee.org/articles/the-morality-of-capitalism/ .

[256] Donald Billings and E. Barry Asmus, "The Morality of Capitalism," Foundation for Economic Education, September 1, 1985, https://fee.org/articles/the-morality-of-capitalism/ .

[257] Donald Billings and E. Barry Asmus, "The Morality of Capitalism," Foundation for Economic Education, September 1, 1985, https://fee.org/articles/the-morality-of-capitalism/ .

[258] Austin Hill and Scott Rae, *The Virtues of Capitalism: A Moral Case for Free Markets* (Chicago, IL: Northfield Publishing, 2010), pp. 48 – 49.

[259] Gerard Francis Lameiro, *America's Economic War – Your Freedom, Money and Life: A Citizen's Handbook for Understanding the War between American Capitalism and Socialism* (Fort Collins, CO: Gerard Francis Lameiro, Ph.D., 2009), pp. 73 – 79.

[260] Julian Adorney, "Actually Bernie, Markets, Not Socialism, Promote Kindness," Foundation for Economic Education, March 21, 2016, https://fee.org/articles/actually-bernie-markets-promote-kindness-not-government/ .

[261] Leslie Albrecht, "Fewer Americans are donating to charity — and it may have nothing to do with money," MarketWatch, December 3, 2019, Copyright MarketWatch, Inc. 2019, https://www.marketwatch.com/story/fewer-americans-are-giving-money-to-charity-and-it-could-be-because-theyre-spending-less-time-at-church-2019-10-28 .

[262] Leslie Albrecht, "Fewer Americans are donating to charity — and it may have nothing to do with money," MarketWatch, December 3, 2019, Copyright MarketWatch, Inc. 2019, https://www.marketwatch.com/story/fewer-americans-are-giving-money-to-charity-and-it-could-be-because-theyre-spending-less-time-at-church-2019-10-28 .

[263] Leslie Albrecht, "The U.S. is the No. 1 most generous country in the world for the last decade," MarketWatch, December 3, 2019, Copyright MarketWatch, Inc. 2019, https://www.marketwatch.com/story/the-us-is-the-most-generous-country-but-americans-say-debt-is-keeping-them-from-giving-more-to-charity-2019-10-18 .

[264] Austin Hill and Scott Rae, *The Virtues of Capitalism: A Moral Case for Free Markets* (Chicago, IL: Northfield Publishing, 2010), pp. 45 -48.

[265] Austin Hill and Scott Rae, *The Virtues of Capitalism: A Moral Case for Free Markets* (Chicago, IL: Northfield Publishing, 2010), pp. 45 -48.

[266] Austin Hill and Scott Rae, *The Virtues of Capitalism: A Moral Case for Free Markets* (Chicago, IL: Northfield Publishing, 2010), pp. 45 -48.

[267] Johan Norberg, In Defense of Global Capitalism (Washington, DC: Cato Institute, 2003), p. 128.

[268] For more information on the relationship between free trade and world peace, you might consider these references: (1) Ludwig von Mises, *Human Action: A Treatise on Economics,* Third Revised Edition (Chicago, IL: Contemporary Books, Inc., Third Edition published by Henry Regnery Company in 1966, Revised Edition, Copyright ©1963 by Yale University, Copyright © 1949 by Yale University Press), pp. 821-832, and (2) Joan Kennedy Taylor, Editor, Free Trade: The Necessary Foundation for World Peace (Irvington-on-Hudson, NY: The Foundation for Economic Education, Inc., 1996).

[269] For more information on single-payer healthcare, please see, for example, Sally C. Pipes, *The False Promise of Single-Payer Health Care* (New York: Encounter Books, 2018).

[270] For more information, you might consider these references: (1) Marc Morano, *The Politically Incorrect Guide ®to Climate Change* (Washington, DC: Regnery Publishing, A Division of Salem Media Group, 2018), and (2) Bruce C. Bunker, *The Mythology of Global Warming: Climate Change Fiction vs. Scientific Facts* (Abbeville, SC: Moonshine Cove Publishing, LLC, 2018).

[271] Tsvetana Paraskova, "The U.S. Just Became A Net Oil Exporter For The First Time Ever," Oilprice.com, December 5, 2019, https://oilprice.com/Energy/Crude-Oil/The-US-Just-Became-A-Net-Oil-Exporter-For-The-First-Time-Ever.html# .

[272] Tsvetana Paraskova, "The U.S. Just Became A Net Oil Exporter For The First Time Ever," Oilprice.com, December 5, 2019, https://oilprice.com/Energy/Crude-Oil/The-US-Just-Became-A-Net-Oil-Exporter-For-The-First-Time-Ever.html# .
[273] Ronald Reagan, "Quotable Quote," goodreads.com, Copyright 2019 by Goodreads, Inc., https://www.goodreads.com/quotes/719383-socialism-only-works-in-two-places-heaven-where-they-don-t .
[274] 2 Corinthians 3:17.
[275] Thomas Jefferson, *Thomas Jefferson: Writings* (New York, NY: The Library of America, Literary Classics of the United States, Inc. 1984), p. 122.

Made in the USA
Middletown, DE
05 August 2020